THE SOUTHERN W

CW00556952

CONTENTS

© Kevin Robertson (Noodle Books) and the various contributors 2009

ISBN 978-1-906419-17-2

First published in 2009 by Kevin Robertson

under the **NOODLE BOOKS** imprint

PO Box 279

Corhampton

SOUTHAMPTON

SO32 3ZX

www.noodlebooks.co.uk

Printed in England by

Ian Allan Printing Ltd

Hersham, Surrey

Editorial Introduction

For the start of this issue I can do little more than repeat what others have kindly reported in the past, "...just where is all the material being published nowadays coming from?" I would never attempt to be so blasé as to imagine such comment referred just to 'SW', for there has been any number of wonderfully researched and comprehensive book and magazine subjects that have appeared recently and I can only assume it is because material that had in the past been contained in private collections is now becoming more accessible.

From my own experience also, I would confirm this trend. The generation older than I had the opportunity to record as well as collect material relative to the steam era railway. Personally I was born perhaps just a few years too late, but that does not mean some earlier material is now always becoming accessible. Please, if you have a friend who fits into the senior category, make sure their paperwork archive is not thrown away. We have all heard the stories of photographs and negatives discarded "as no-one is interest nowadays," but we certainly are! I experienced this myself with a drawfull of pre-grouping railway tickets discarded just 24 hours before I was due to visit a collection.

A recent edition of the BBC 'Antiques Roadshow' featured a man with a railway nameplate. The presenter commented to the effect that prices for such items had peaked, as those with an interest were slowly becoming fewer. Inevitably that is no doubt the case, but whilst family and friends will no doubt accept there is some value in hardware and models, photographs,

paperwork and even old railway files and observations can be equally valuable, even if not in pure financial terms.

I have never owned a nameplate in my life. Yes of course I would love one, whether 'she that must be obeyed' would approve, is another matter. I know the last time I bought an 'O' gauge model I was greeted with three questions (she recognised the wooden box), "What is it, why do you need it and how much did it cost?". That little spending spree cost me dearly she changed her car. I dread to think what the equivalent peace offering would be for a nameplate.

Where is this leading? Well, simply, I personally obtain just as much pleasure from having access to historic paperwork and photographs as a splendid piece of brasswork. It matters not what the company is, the important thing is that those records are not lost. Personally, I am not totally sure I approve of seeing photo collections split either, but sometimes there are good reasons for so doing. There are of course any number of worthy museums, auction houses and even railway societies who will handle railway-related items.

With so much material thus appearing it was interesting to be asked the question the other day, will I be producing an equivalent 'SW' for any other company? Here the answer is an emphatic 'No', but somebody should. The LNER especially cries out for such attention. Whether 'Great North of Scotland Way' would be commercially viable however, is perhaps another question altogether.

Kevin Robertson

...and now for something completely different...

Now you see why for this issue we have changed the format to include the accompanying view, on, of course, 'Page 3'.

Before you ask, YES, IT IS RAILWAY RELATED and YES, ALL WILL BE REVEALED, (well some of it at least) on page 23.

No, we have not increased the print run for this issue either, but I did promise you something different for Issue 7......extra pages of course!

(I totally refuse to say whose idea this all was.)

Left - Waterloo, undated, (we would suspect late Southern / early BR) but wonderfully evocative. The law is watching.......

(RCHS - Spence collection)

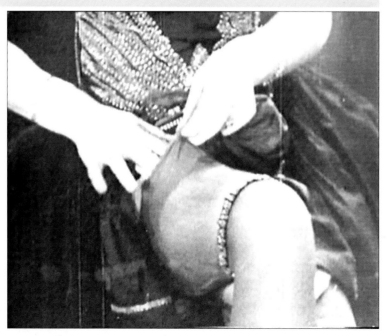

Opened as the Callington branch of the Plymouth and Devonport South Western Junction Railway on 2nd March 1908, PDSWJR survived as an independent concern until 30th November 1922. For a very short time it was then in the ownership of the LSWR before being taken over by the Southern Railway at the grouping. The branch origins can be traced back to May 1872 with an original line from Calstock Quay, via a cable operated incline, to Kelly Bray a mile from Callington. Takeover by the PDSWJR occurred in 1891 although it was only consequent upon Light Railways Orders of 1900 and 1905 that the route was converted from its original 3' 6" gauge to the standard gauge and also extended via a 129' high stone viaduct across the Tamar to join the PDSWJR main line in a north-facing connection at Bere Alston. The views depict, above, the viaduct and below, c1906, the down side approach embankment under construction. In the top view, c1907, is the contractor, Messrs. Lang's, locomotive 'Blanch' with tipping wagons. See also page 21.

THE CALLINGTON BRANCH

History and Memories

John Snell

At the end of 1948 I was about to leave school and wanted to work on the railway. Living at Gunnislake, which had a station on the Bere Alston to Callington branch line, I wrote to the Southern Region's Western District Office at Exeter Central Station . The good news was that they were recruiting clerical staff and provided I could pass a written examination and a medical I had a job.

Initially though, I had to prove my aptitude and so attended the Exeter office for the written examination, followed, a few weeks later, by a medical. Even though I was headed for a clerk's job we were still tested for colour blindness which was achieved by picking out numbers from a book. The reason for this, was, from the clerical grades promotion could be had to the operating department.

At this time, working between Exeter St Davids and Exeter Central, there was a retired railway man and a dog. The dog carried a barrel on his back collecting for The Southern Orphanage at Woking. Indeed between 1942 and 1951 just over £11,000 was collected for this worthy cause. For many years there was a plaque outside Exeter Central station commemorating 'The Children's Friends'; two dogs were involved, 'Nigger' and 'Sandy'. (When you joined the railway you were invited to allow 6d per week to be deducted from your pay for the Southern Railway Orphanage; most employees did this.)

Having been successful with the examination and medical, I had to report again to the Exeter District Office, this time to be interviewed by the District Superintendent, Mr George Bishop, whilst I was to learn that any correspondence to this individual was to be addressed, G Bishop Esq.

I was just 15 years old when Mr Bishop

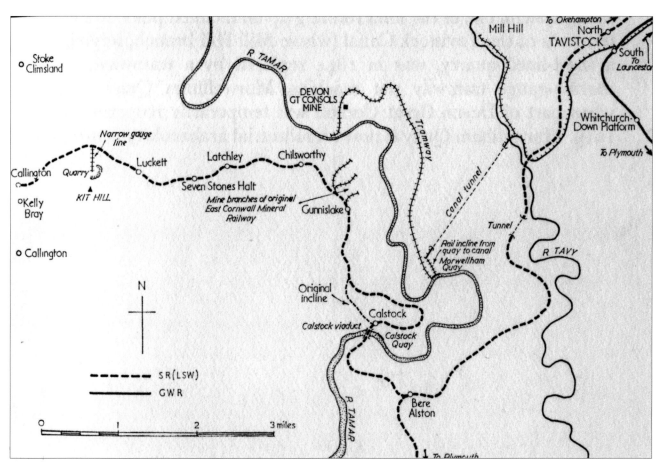

Captioned on the original print as, 'The building of the railway station at Kelly Bray', this is more likely to refer to the construction or a possible extension to the station at Callington itself. The men are employees of Messrs Dingle's sawmills. Work on converting the old line as well as the building of the extension to Bere Alston commenced in 1904 and was undertaken by John C Lang, a building contractor from Liskeard. It is likely he would also have used local men as shown here.

addressed me. His position from behind a huge desk being somewhat daunting. I recall I was advised, "...we are taking you on the railway and there are two things you must understand. One, never permit any slackness in the care of the company's cash and two, never get out of a moving train. Now I want you to report to the Station Master at Calstock to learn clerical duties.......".

Duly I reported to Mr Tubb, the Calstock Station Master on 4th April 1949. Mr Tubb was not just in charge at one station, as his area included Calstock, Gunnislake and Chilsworthy Halt. At the end of the branch at Callington, Mr Lazenbury was the Station Master and he similarly had charge of Callington, Luckett and Latchley. Meanwhile at Bere Alston, the junction for the branch, it

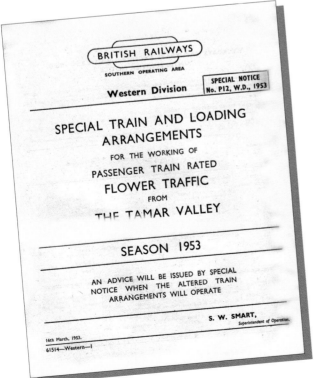

was Mr Skinner.

At the time I started, April, it was right in the busy Flower and Fruit season. This lasted from early February to July, during which time, on average, some 400,000 packages would leave the Tamar Valley for up-country markets. At Calstock the gardens were south facing and produced early crops, which fetched top money. Daffodils were sent first, followed by Iris then the famous Tamar Valley Double Whites, finally strawberries and raspberries.

The growers would present consignment notes, which detailed their traffic. This had to be charged and waybills made out to the destination station. Flower boxes weighed seven pounds each, thus sixteen equalled one hundredweight. At the time sending 1 cwt to Waterloo cost 10s. Accounts were sent to the growers weekly and payments had to be accounted for.

The railway provided three trains from Callington for this traffic. These were the 9.43 am destined for the northern markets; Glasgow, Edinburgh, Newcastle, Manchester, Liverpool and Leeds: the 1.00 pm from Callington for Midlands traffic; Birmingham, Wolverhampton, Derby, Leicester, Coventry, Nottingham, Chesterfield and Sheffield: and the 4.23 pm from Callington for traffic to London, Bristol, Newport, Cardiff, Swansea, and Tonypandy. All this traffic was sent station to station, excepting that destined for London where it was delivered direct from Waterloo to the Covent Garden, Spitalfields and the Borough Markets. Understandably, as this traffic was perishable it was a hands-on operation for all concerned. In January each year the railway would take the leading growers to a lunch at the Rougemont Hotel, Exeter. First class passes would be given for their travel.

In Southern Railway days traffic for the North and Midlands were routed from Bere Alston to Templecombe and thence Bath over the old Somerset and Dorset route, thus avoiding the GWR. Bere Alston would telegraph the van numbers for transfer and would also telegraph Waterloo the number of packages for delivery. This arrangement lasted until the lines west of Exeter were transferred to the Western Region after which the North and Midland destinations were routed via Exeter St Davids and Bristol.

At Bere Alston there was a Midland Railway house where their agent lived. He worked in Plymouth canvassing traffic for the Midland railway via Templecombe and Bath. The fruit and flower industry was big and it was an important source of revenue for the railway. Today it is hard to imagine all the traffic sent from the Callington line and Bere Alston.

In addition to flowers and fruit, other traffic was milk in churns. These were loaded in a van on the 9.43 am from Callington: 8 churns at Callington, 2 at Luckett, 16 at Gunnislake, 2 at Calstock and 2 at Bere Alston. The van would then be attached to the 10.30 am train at Bere Alston destined for the Plymouth Co-op at Friary station.

At Calstock there was a chip basket factory and these were forwarded weekly to Evesham and also to Kent. The factory always thought they were hard done by , as the vans used for this traffic had a capacity of 12 tons whilst the baskets when loaded, came to just 10 cwt. On the basis of space used the railway had to maintain a charge of 2 tons!

In season, trucks of cider apples were despatched to Whiteways, the cider makers at Whimple. Another regular forwarding was pit props from the Duke of Bedford's woods at Gunnislake; these would go to the mines in the north of England and also to South Wales.

Callington also sent cattle specials at regular intervals. Thursdays at Bere Alston, Mr Bolt of Rumleigh Farm would send boxes of day old chicks. These had to be route labelled, for example, on a box destined for Newquay, the label would read 'Bere Alston to Newquay via Plymouth and Par'. Finally, Hingston Down Quarry might despatch 20 hoppers of stone between Monday to Friday, consequently the line was very busy.

Received traffic included, of course, coal. Local coal merchants were Perry Spears and the Plymouth Co-op at Bere Alston, Fred Jury at Calstock, Wescotts and Pine Bros at Gunnislake and the Co-op at Callington, all of whom had depots in the respective yards. Animal feed came from Avonmouth, Lyon's cakes and ice cream were received as well as fresh fish in wooden boxes from Grimsby destined for the local fishmongers. Additionally there were GPO mail and daily news papers, all by train.

Also at Calstock some 70 wagons of timber per year arrived from Scandinavia for the chip basket factory. As the railway yard here was small and could only deal with 10 wagons at a time, a timber gang would arrive complete with mobile crane, road vehicle and trailer. In this way the timber could be quickly off-loaded and delivered to the factory which was located near to the station. Each station also had a delivery agent, Ambrose Brown at Bere Alston, Ken Worth at Calstock, Pine Bros

Seen from the Devon side, a view of the first train crossing the viaduct behind 'A.S. Harris' and on its way to Bere Alston. The stock was second-hand 4-wheel coaches. Between Bere Alson and Calstock, 59,300 cu.yds. of spoil had to be removed. Between Calstock to just below Albaston the figure was 66,000 of which 41,000 came from Harewood cutting. In the background is the wagon hoist.

Rectory Footbridge, the only wooden bridge on the line and although 2½ miles from Calstock Church was provided for the Calstock Rector to walk safely between his Rectory and Church. The timber was always painted white and as such stood out as such in the valley. The actual Rectory was relocated in the village of Calstock in 1952 consequent upon which the bridge was removed. (Records indicate that this was one of 11 bridges on the line whose numbers and distance from Bere Alston were as follows, 1 - Bere Alston, stone construction. 2 - Iron Deck, approximately ¼ mile from Bere Alston. 3 - Stone, ½ mile from Helstone near Bere Alston. 4 - Stone, 1¼ miles at North Ward near Bere Alston. 5 - Calstock Viaduct at 1¼ miles. 6 - Iron deck ,1¾ miles, Church Hill Calstock. 7 - Stone, 2 miles, Harewood near Calstock. 8 - Rectory Footbridge seen above. 9 - Stone, 2¾ miles, Church Town, Calstock. 10 - Stone, 3¼ miles, near Adbaston. 11 - Stone, 4 miles, near Adbaston.)

at Gunnislake, and Fred Rogers at Callington.

Working on the railway we never knew when the travelling auditor might arrive. These were senior staff dark suits with a brief-case; fussy suspicious people, they would examine all the station records. Once at Bere Alston one auditor started to examine the parcel delivery sheets. He quickly noted many of the signatures, although of different names, were made in similar writing. The local explanation was simple, that during the busy flower season there would be no one at home and the delivery agent Mr Brown referred to above, would leave a parcel in a discreet place and then sign the person's name on the sheet himself. The auditor asked the railway staff for an explanation but could not get a satisfactory answer. (The staff all knew what was happening, but did not want to get Mr Brown in trouble). Consequently the auditor asked to

see Mr Brown when he arrived for the day's parcels. Mr Brown was a typical village character and when asked for his account pondered for a while before coming out with , "Sir I can explain why the signatures are similar, the reason is they all went to the same school!"

July 1950 saw a large increase of goods traffic on the branch. The Royal Cornwall Show was held at Callington and consequently trains had to be double-headed. Before this, in April 1950, Bere Alston and all stations on the Callington line were visited by Chief Inspector Paye from Waterloo. Mr Paye took notes on the length of the platforms and sidings which we found out later was in case the Royal Train were to travel on the branch. It never did, but the Royal party did attend the show. Instead, the Royal Train took them to Saltash from where they went by road to Callington. Even so there was

Right - Whilst the PDSWJR owned the line from Lydford to Devonport, this was always worked by the LSWR using LSWR motive power. For working the Callington branch however, the company ordered three tank engines, two 0-6-2Ts and an 0-6-0T. All were named. Here 'Earl of Mount Edgcumbe' is temporarily minus driving wheels at Plymouth Friary on 12th July 1924, but sports evidence of LSWR ownership. The two larger tank engines remained at work on their line until the early 1950s when ousted by newer Ivatt 2-6-2Ts. Even so it was not quite the end, for the pair found their way to Eastleigh , and E757, by now 30757, was the last of the PDSW engines to remain in service, being withdrawn in December 1957.

Calstock station looking towards Bere Alston, c1908.

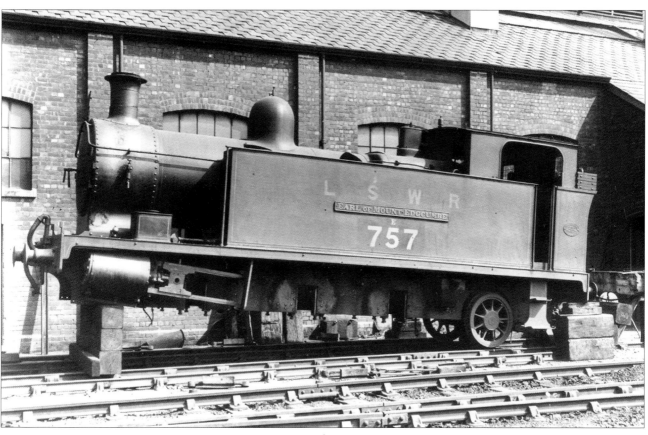

Latchley station, circa 1910. At the time, Mrs Jenkins, far right, was the Station Mistress in charge - did the LSWR use that term? The station was the former Cox Park Depot on the East Cornwall Mineral Railway.

a railway connection. At the time the station master at Callington, Mr Lazenbury, was the Portreeve (Mayor) of Callington and Mr Lazenbury had the duty and privilege of greeting King George and Queen Elizabeth together with the two Princesses to the show ground. The Southern Railway had always encouraged its staff to serve on local councils.

Having started at Calstock in April 1949, in August I was transferred to Gunnislake. This was fine with me as Gunnislake was where I lived. It was though a short lived bonus as a year later, in August 1950, I was transferred again, this time to the junction station at Bere Alston. I also now had to work both early and late turns, 6.00 a.m.- 2.00 pm, 2.00 p.m. -10.00 p.m. Bere Alston was also seven miles away and I used to cycle, much of it uphill. Dependent upon the shift, I would leave home at 5.00 a.m. whilst on late turn I would get home at 11.00 p.m. There was also a requirement to work every other Sunday.

At this time on the branch on weekdays, around 250 passengers travelled, whilst from Bere Alston that figure was 350. Many men worked in Devonport Dockyard and for them we issued workmen's tickets up to 7.30 a.m. After this it was cheap day tickets to 11.30 a.m. and finally half-day tickets. The respective return fares from Bere Alston to Plymouth in 1950 were 2/3d, 2/9d and 1/9d. Season Tickets were also popular, these could be weekly, monthly and three-monthly, mainly to St Budeaux, Ford, Devonport, Plymouth and Tavistock.

At Bere Alston an unusual season ticket was issued. This was from Bere Alston to Leamington Spa, in the name of Mr Dorey who worked for Thomas Motors in Plymouth. Mr Dorey would use it to travel to the midlands Sundays to Fridays and then drive a new car back to Plymouth. This cost £32 monthly.

Up to the late 1940s there were Party Fields at Bere Ferrers and Bere Alston. Parties, mainly Sunday Schools from Plymouth, would have an outing to these fields. I have records of 1,000 passengers arriving at Bere Ferrers. At the fields there would be swing boats, swings, donkey rides and lovely Devonshire cream teas. In the flower season children would always take a bunch of flowers back to their mother. Understandably these were very popular events.

In 1935 the Southern Railway had introduced Holiday Camping Coaches in the Tamar Valley area, one coach being placed at Brentor, no doubt for the lovers of Dartmoor and another coach at Gunnislake station. They were advertised as 'Happy Holidays'. The following year a coach was also berthed at Bere Ferrers. All main line companies had these coaches and by 1938 some 10,000 families were enjoying such holidays. By today's standards however, facilities were rudimentary. Most had eight berths, with oil for both cooking and lighting. Water had to obtained from the local station and the station toilets used. The station staff were responsible for changing the linen on Saturdays ready for the new arrivals. A condition imposed when the booking was made, was that the party travelled to and from the site by train. Despite all of this, they proved very popular. The cost for

Calstock, April 1955 and busy times during the flower season. Porter Albert Harris is on the platform and Relief Signalman Frank Chard in the doorway.

a week in 1935 varied according to the season and was from £2.10s to £3.10s. The vehicles could be booked from early April to the first week in October. Despite the outbreak of war in September 1939 the season was continued until October, but the vehicles were then withdrawn. Following, some of the stock was refitted and used as ambulance vehicles for the duration.

The service was not reinstated until mid-1954 although now it was only Bere Ferrers in the Tamar valley that offered the facility. Certainly by 1960 two such camping coaches were based at the station and I found myself involved to some extent when working there. This was in helping the arriving holidaymakers who had ordered groceries for their arrival. I would telephone the local baker, Mr Hughes, who would deliver the items to the coach.

Railway staff were encouraged to attend Rules and Regulation classes and First Aid classes. At Bere Alston, during the winter months, Rules and Regulation classes were held on Monday evenings and First Aid classes were held on Thursday evenings. All grades attended and it was much like a social occasion. Mr Skinner, the Bere Alston Station Master, took the Monday class and Doctor Trowbridge from Callington, took the Thursday class. At the end of the sessions, exams were taken and upon passing, certificates were presented to the staff. The First Aid class always held an annual dinner when their certificates were presented. In both instances a high-ranking officer would make the presentation.

Mr Skinner would also arrange visits to various depots on the Southern. I recall a trip to Feltham Marshalling yard and seeing the large G16 Urie 4-8-0T

'hump shunting'. On other occasions we went to Waterloo Signal Box and the Clapham Junction signalling school. On these long distance trips, we travelled overnight on the Saturday 12.00 midnight Plymouth to Paddington where Mr Skinner would book breakfasts before continuing to our destination. Mr Skinner would also take us into a Lyon's Corner House for refreshments. The return was on the Sunday 4.00 p.m. from Waterloo arriving back at Bere Alston at 10.10 p.m.

Station lighting varied. Callington and Bere Alston had electric lights, Luckett, Latchley and Chilsworthy had oil lamps, lit and set out by the train guards. Gunnislake was lit by gas from the Gunnislake Gas Works (all their coal came by train), whilst at Calstock there were Tilley Lamps.

To control the trains, the single line was worked in a variety of ways. Between Bere Alston and Calstock, 'Staff and Ticket' was in operation, although beyond was electric token. In all cases the instruments were located in the booking office although the points and signals were operated from ground frames.

Due to the inflexibility of working between Calstock and Bere Alston, if a relief signalman was on duty on late turn at Calstock, it was necessary to remind him that the last train of the day, the 9.30 p.m. goods from Callington, must go forward to Bere Alston with a ticket, because the next train to Bere Alston was the next day's 5.30 am passenger train, Callington to Bere Alston. This service conveyed dockyard workmen.

The signalmen communicated with each other, not by bells but by means of the railway phone, "Is line clear?", "Train entering section" and "Train out of

section" all done this way and the times recorded in the signalman's register. The phone codes were Callington '1-3' Luckett '1-2' Gunnislake '4' Calstock '2' Bere Alston signal box '3' Bere Alston booking office '2-3'. At Bere Alston there was a main line signal box which was open between 5.00 a.m. and 11.00 p.m. Outside these times, Bere Alston was switched-out and the section on the main line became Devonport to Tavistock, both of which were 24 hour boxes.

There were times however, when Bere Alston box was open continuously. This was nearly always when the sea wall at Dawlish flooded and the Western would work their trains to Exeter via Bere Alston and Okehampton. To ensure Western drivers retained the necessary route knowledge, the Monday to Saturday 2.35 p.m. stopping train, Plymouth to Exeter, was always worked by a Western engine (Manor or Grange) with Western driver, fireman and guard. On the branch, water was available for the engines at Calstock and Callington, water always being taken at Calstock when running in the Callington direction. Engines usually worked bunker first from Callington to Bere Alston and chimney first in the other direction.

Of the services on the main line, one that sticks in the memory was the 11.10 a.m. Plymouth Friary to Brighton. This train would run through around mid-day, a lovely sight, 10 coaches, one a restaurant car and hauled by a new 'West Country' engine. It was due to arrive at

Brighton at 5.55 p.m. In the reverse direction, the service from Brighton left at the same time and was due to reach Plymouth at 6.00 p.m. In the down direction only, the service stopped at Bere Alston at 5.36 p.m., mainly to set down office workers from Tavistock. Bere Alston down platform could only accommodate eight coaches so the rear two were off the platform and it was the guard's duty at Tavistock to go through the rear coaches advising passengers if they wished to alight at Bere Alston to please move forward.

On one occasion during the flower season Mr Sherrell, who was a leading grower, was unloading his flowers for dispatch when the up Brighton ran through. The porter Ronald was helping him. Mr Sherrell asked, "What train is that, Ron?" "That's the Brighton, Mr Sherrell." "What time does it get to Brighton?" Ronald did not know the time, but his reply was, "I don't know, but it can't take very long because it's back here again around half past five." Of course that was the down Brighton, the two services having crossed each other near to Yeovil Junction. When that story got around, Ron's leg was pulled many times.

Another train was the 4.40 p.m. Plymouth Friary to Waterloo which ran via Eastleigh, arriving at Waterloo at 3.48 a.m. The train was formed with coaches, PMV's, more coaches and more parcel vans. The vans were mainly newspaper vans working back to London. There was also naval traffic working between Devonport and Portsmouth.

Opposite, top: *Locomotives outside and alongside the shed at the terminus of the line at Callington - geographically perhaps more accurately named Kelly Bray, 27th June 1956. The Ivatt tank types appeared in BR days No 41306 had migrated west from Three Bridges in late spring 1955, 30192, an '02' 0-4-4T seen taking water, was Plymouth based and remained in the West Country until withdrawn in August 1961.*

Opposite, bottom: *LSWR vestibule First / Third composite, No S6558S, once the coach portion of an LSWR steam-railmotor vehicle and then later part of a push-pull set, seen inside the train shed at Callington complete with a PMV. Reference to the carriage working diagram on the next page reveals this was likely to have been a morning service. Accommodation was for six 1st class passengers next to the Guard's compartment, and 48 3rd class. The iron gates segregated the two types of accommodation.*

Callington (Weekdays) Commencing 8th June 1953 UFN					
a.m. 5.20	Bere Alston	1 bke cpo.(C.A.) 2-set 361 }		Berth	
7.09 SO 7.16 SX }	Bere Alston Plymouth Friary	2-set "A" 1 P.M.V. (4) }		Berth	
9.44	Plymouth Friary Bere Alston	1 P.M.V. (4) 2-set "A"	8.24 a.m.	Berth Bere Alston	9.08
p.m. 1.00	Bere Alston	2-set "A"	10.50 a.m.	Bere Alston	11.34
4.23	Bere Alston Gunnislake	2-set "A" P & P set SO {	3.15 p.m. 3.22 p.m. 1.02 p.m.	Bere Alston Bere Alston Bere Alston	3.57 SX 4.04 SO 1.46 SO
6.20	Bere Alston	2-set "A"	5.23 a.m.	Bere Alston	6.05
9.10 SO	Bere Alston	2-set "A"	7.10 p.m.	Bere Alston	7.53
	Berth	2 P.M.V. (4) {	3.15 p.m. 3.22 p.m.	Bere Alston Bere Alston	3.57 SX 4.04 SO
	Berth	1 bke.cpo (C.A.) SX 2-set 361 SO }	5.23 p.m.	Bere Alston	6.05
SX	Berth	2-set "A"	7.10 p.m.	Bere Alston	7.53
SX	Berth	2-set 361	8.00 p.m.	Bere Alston	8.42
SO	Berth	2-set "A" 1 bke.cpo (C.A.) }	10.05	Bere Alston	10.49
2 coach set "A" is formed of 2 trailer bke. Compos.					

The train ran non-stop Devonport to Bere Alston always signalled from Bere Ferrers under Regulation 5, (Section clear but station blocked). After leaving Bere Alston it stopped at every station to Salisbury.

The 'ACE' was an important train which did not stop at Bere Alston and passed through in the down direction around 4.05 p.m. At this stage, this working was no more than two coaches hauled by a 'N' class locomotive, having left Waterloo at 11.00 a.m. The 'ACE' was the most multi-portion train to run in the UK. From Waterloo there would be through coaches for Seaton, Sidmouth, Exmouth, Exeter, Torrington, Ilfracombe, Padstow, Bude and Plymouth. Sir John Betjeman used to travel by this train to his holidays in North Cornwall. In his book 'Summoned by Bells' he wrote, "Attended the long express at Waterloo that takes us down to Cornwall, tea time shows, the small fields waiting, every blackthorn edge straining inland before the south west gale. The emptying train, wind in the ventilators puffs out of Egloskerry to Tresmeer, through minty meadows under bearded trees and hills upon whose slopes the clinging farms hold Bible Christians. Can this be the same carriage that came from Waterloo. On Wadebridge station what a breath of sea scented the Camel Valley. Cornish air and soft Cornish rain and silence after steam. Can this be the same carriage that came from Waterloo? Waterloo a busy terminus in our nations capital and Wadebridge station, a busy station but a country one."

THE BIG FREEZE, 1963

"I well remember this event, on Saturday 29th December 1962 I was the late turn booking clerk at Bere Alston. Snow had started falling around 10.00 am and it continued all day. The early afternoon trains were running reasonably to time but by 6.00 pm blizzard conditions prevailed and services were very late.

"I should have been off at 10.00 pm but was still on duty at 11.30 pm dealing with late running trains to Plymouth and Tavistock. I was then told by the stationmaster, Mr Skinner, to go home, because I was due back on duty at 8.50 am on Sunday. Show was falling heavily as I walked the mile back home, mostly also over my knees.

"Reporting for duty the next day I learnt all services were suspended with three trains snowed in near Okehampton. The next day I was again on duty, this time at 6.00 am, but an emergency service had been arranged between Tavistock and Plymouth for Dockyard and shop workers. On top of that the electricity failed and I was issue with an oil lamp to book passengers.

"The six weeks that the line was closed alerted the authorities to how vulnerable our line was to weather conditions, despite traffic levels being high: the forced closure did nothing to assist our case with Dr Beeching."

Gunnislake Station 15th September 1962. Ivatt 2-6-2T No 41216, left, in charge of the 1.00 pm Callington to Bere Alston whilst sister engine No 41214, approaches with the Saturday only, 1.00 pm Bere Alston to Callington service. Gunnislake was the only intermediate crossing place where passenger trains were permitted to cross.

PRIVATE SIDINGS - all with a gate and ground frame unlocked by the respective single line token / staff.

PEARSON'S QUARRY, GUNISLAKE

Located at the Chilsworthy end of Gunnislake Station, to the right of the present day road bridge off Station Road. The route then took it under a bridge that took a lane into Sand Hill House, opposite the Catholic Church, thence the rails ran down Body's Court into the quarry. Within the quarry the rails also ran over a series of large pillars to reach the smaller Hardwell Quarry. Originally built to the East Cornwall Mineral Railways' 3'6" gauge, standard gauge was adopted from March 1908. Within the quarry, 'Ada', the former Devon Great Consol mine engine was used to haul granite to Gunnislake Station. Most of the sidings were removed circa 1915 but parts of the line could still be seen at Pearson's Quarry in the 1940s. In the period prior to the latter date, I recall my mother occasionally taking a pasty to my grandfather who worked as a stone cutter.

REFUGE SIDING, 4m 5ch, between CALSTOCK and GUNNISLAKE. (All distances measured from Bere Alston).

Serving Drakewalls Mine, this facility was removed in 1910.

PERRY SPEARS SIDING, 4m 5 ch, between CALSTOCK and GUNNISLAKE

On the down side of the line with a facing connection for down trains (defined as those travelling from Bere Alston to Callington). The firm of Perry Spears was a well known local organisation who had its headquarters at Tavistock. The firm dealt with coal, manure, animal feed and lime. The yard was taken over by Messrs Wescotts Coal Merchants in the late 1940s with Mr Dixon as the Manager. By 1960 Cecil Kerslake was Manager. Wagons destined for the site were first sent to Callington and then marshalled next to the engine for the return so as to be easily detached and shunted. A catch point within the siding, 37 yards from the main line, protected vehicles standing inside. The siding was removed in 1966 with the site now occupied by the relocated 1994 Gunnislake Station.

SANDHILL PARK SIDING, 4m 66ch, between GUNNISLAKE and CHILSWORTHY

Situated just beyond Gunnislake Station and facing up trains. Originally provided for Messrs Cocking and Son's brickworks it later became Symons' coal yard. (Mr Symons had a coal yard at Cothele Quay but when the station at Bere Alston opened in 1890 he transferred his business there. With the opening of the Callington Branch he transferred to the Sandhill Park site.) Wagons were placed in the siding by trains working in the down direction. Due to a steep 1 in 35 gradient from the running line for a distance of about 85 yards, two catch points were provided, the innermost one operated by a hand-lever. There was short section of level line leading to a set of stop blocks although it was a requirement that vehicles left in the siding be 'scotched'. Staff recalled as working at the site in the 1940s were Jim Richards and Tom Edwards. At the end of this decade, Jack and Wilfred Pine took over the business. The siding was removed in 1951.

GREEN HILL SIDINGS, 5m 24ch, between Gunnislake and Chilsworthy.

The siding was on the down side of the line facing up trains. Three separate commodities were dealt with; brick, arsenic and chemicals. Sulphuric acid and arsenic were produced and sent out in sealed railway vans. A set of catch points were provided 42 yards from the main line. The siding was out of use in 1934 and removed in 1948.

HILL WESTLAKE SIDINGS, 5m 44ch, between Chilsworthy and Latchley.

On the down side and facing down trains. Originally a brickworks, but taken over in 1942 by the Government as an Emergency Food Store depot, known to railwaymen as 'The Buffer Depot'. In charge was Mrs Jones, assisted by Mr Murton and Cecil Murray. The siding was removed in 1955.

WHITE ROCKS SIDINGS, 6m 13ch, and HINGSTONE DOWN SIDING, 6m 24ch, between Chilsworthy and Latchley.

Both of these sidings served the Hingston Down Quarry. White Rocks was on the down side of the line facing up trains. Opened on 3rd November 1925 it was in use for several decades but taken up on 23rd September 1962. Hingston Down was also on the down side of the line and had a loop alongside the main line used for shunting into any of several sidings within the quarry. A set of catch points stood 66 yards from the main line. Additionally a line was provided to the Council

Quarry, opened in 1905 to help in alleviating unemployment in Calstock Parish, and which was located just below the Hingston Down quarry. Hingston Down sidings were the last to be used on the branch and were in use up to the early 1960s. The lines were finally removed in 1966.

KIT HILL SIDING, 8m 43ch, between Luckett and Callington.

On the down side of the line with a connection facing up trains. This served a quarry of the same name by means of a rope-worked incline, the power for which came from a stationary steam engine at the top of the incline. In the 1940s, Herbert Trebilcock was in charge of this engine. The actual quarry was owned by William Griffith and Co. and was renowned for the production of large pieces of polished granite. The quarry closed in 1955 and the lines were removed.

Pre 1908 sidings. In East Cornwall Mineral Railway ownership days, there were also sidings for the Plymouth Fire Clay brickworks at Middle Dimson, Gunnislake - the pillars which once carried the railway over the road between Gunnislake and North Dimson can still be seen. Sidings were also provided for the Phoenix brickworks at Latchley. Both of these facilities ceased to exist prior to March 1908.

In July 1950 the Royal Cornwall show was held at Callington. Due to the increase in traffic trains had to be double-headed, 'Earl of Mount Edgecumbe' and 'Lord St Levan' are seen near Sandway's Crossing between Calstock and Gunnislake.

In the same year, 1950, yet still displaying Southern ownership in BR days. No 758 'Lord St Levan' waiting to depart from Gunnislake for Bere Alston with a fruit special. On the footplate are, left - Fireman Ron Nicholls and Driver Bill Symons. Ron Pote, the Gunnislake Porter / Signalman is standing by the engine.

A

B

C

A - 30758 'Lord St Levan' shunting at Calstock in April 1955. Tim Wonacott is seen coupling the wagon.

B - Guard Roy Barratsall on the 10.15 am freight from Callington to Bere Alston, seen at Calstock in April 1955.

C - Jack Thompson loading flowers at Gunnislake, June 1950. Jack was a temporary member of staff hired for the fruit and flower season between February and July.

D - Calstock station April 1955. Left - Porter Albert Harris and Relief Signalman Frank Chard.

E - Calstock station April 1955. Left - Porter Les Pote and Signalman Cyril Barnes.

F - Doris Woolcock with daughter Pat, at the railway cottage Latchley in 1939

G - Calstock station 1955. Left - John Snell and Porter Albert Harris.

H - Circa 1950, Les Woolcock and Aubrey Down load animal feed at Latchley destined for Bertie Hearn's poultry farm.

D

E

Snapshots from the branch

← F

G →

H
↓

Callington circa 1956. Mr Chamber, Station Master Callington, has been promoted to Station Master Watchet and is being presented with an electric fire by Mr Skinner, the Station Master at Bere Alston.

Those present are L to R, M Phare, C Johns, W Bryant, R Coombe, J Rickard, Mr Chamber, L Rodda, H Jones, R Rouse, Mr Skinner, L Pote, J Snell, J Raynor, W Simmons and W Jarvis.

Callington Staff 1950. Left to right; **Back row***; S Davis, Guard; J Wickett, Driver; Bill Bryant, Driver; Bill Symons, Porter; C Burrows, Engineers Dept; R Osbourne, Porter; J Raynor, Porter.* **Middle row** *left to right: B Mugridge, Fireman; R Woods, Fireman; G Cullis, Engineers Dept; L Pote, Porter; G Hunn, Ganger; B Stephens, Porter.* **Front row** *left to right; J Osborne, Guard; R Thaies, Guard; J Friend, Fireman; Bill May, Driver in charge*; Mr Lazenby, Station Master; R Coombes, Signalman; C Gould, Goods Foreman; J Jury, Signalman; N Rundle, Porter / Signalman. (* Bill May was Driver in Charge from PDSWJR days. He was paid 1/- a week more than other drivers.*

Right - Luckett Station, circa 1961. the empty wagons in the loop were for Hingsdown Quarry.

Above - The top of Kit Hill Quarry incline. Wagons from Luckett were hauled up by a stationary steam engine. In the 1940s, Herbert Trebilcock was in charge.

Right - Gunnislake June 1950, recorded by Charlie Dommett,Relief Porter; who lived at Brentor. L to R, John Snell, Clerk; Rex Phillips, Signalman; Jock Thompson, Temporary porter; George Symes, Porter / Signalman; Ron Pote, Porter / Signalman; George Jury Signalman.

Calstock Wagon lift

When the railway was opened in March 1908, at the Calstock end of the viaduct a wagon lift was erected to provide access to the quay. The lift was one of the highest in England at 113 feet above the Quay.

The lift was designed by Messrs Galbraith and Church of the LSWR and installed by Head Wrightson & Co, the foundations being provided by the viaduct builder, John Lang.

The cage and framework of the lift were comprised entirely of mild steel forming strongly braced structures with an ample margin of strength. The cage could hold one four-wheeled open wagon of 15 tons gross weight. The motive power for raising and lowering the cage was a steam boiler and winding engine fixed to the top of the lift framing. Duplicate steel ropes were provided to raise the cage. Each of these was capable of holding the load should the other have failed.

The cage was held at the top platform level by a safety securing device. Safety gates at the top and bottom were worked automatically by the cage so that they closed the entrance as soon as it left either level. An electric bell was operated by the cage as it approached its destination.

There was a short approach of steel girders at the top, parallel with the viaduct, along which trucks were pushed. The girders were supported by large concrete plinths which can still be seen. At the lower level the wagon would be hauled out of the cage on to a turntable and turned on to the sidings which ran along the quay. Wagons of granite and bricks used the lift, but as the railway became more popular, the lift was used less.

The structure was taken down in 1934. The 'Western Morning News' of 8th September 1934 contained a brief and prosaic mention and which provided the only obituary of the Calstock wagon hoist installed less than 30 years earlier. The remains were eventually sold as scrap to Germany in 1938.

POSTER TIME

A chance find amongst a collection of Southern-related miscellanea, was a double-sided print the main view of which was clearly a b/w rendition of the SECR poster seen left. Possibly of even greater interest however, was that of the reverse which was a copy of the original photograph before being 'doctored' in the style of the period for the poster. Purely from a personal perspective, but a view seemingly shared by those who viewed this issue in the course of preparation, it seems we all prefer the un-doctored version - possibly a change of fashion almost a century later.

Speaking of dates and this is slightly difficult. A copy, again in black and white, appears on the NRM website, where it is credited as being from 1915. A brief caption there refers to The Garden of England being a popular tourist and day tripper destination. Perfectly true of course, but were such excursions still being run in 1915? The date may of course be correct, Francis Dent, as General Manager of the SECR, being in post between 1911 and 1920.

The child involved, no name is indicated, bears a passing similarity to the images recalled on contemporary Pears Soap adverts, perhaps a starlet of the time. Did she likewise feature in later cinema?

Was there also a coloured version? No doubt an SECR expert will reveal all........ .

THE SOUTHERN AND THE SILVER SCREEN

Martin Dean

The newly created Southern Railway was an unhappy organisation. Its management was fragmented because initially there were three General Managers whose remit covered their former pre–grouping lines. Little wonder that policy could not be agreed upon. Throughout 1923 the Board overcame these difficulties until the new railway company was united under the ex-LSWR's General Manager, Sir Herbert Walker. Only then could the necessary actions be started.

However, the problems of the first few months caused much resentment and criticism. The public had been promised an improvement in the quality of their services under the new Southern Railway company and this appeared not to be happening. Even the electrification of the former SECR lines in 1924, which not surprisingly created operational difficulties, exacerbated the situation. The failure of the Southern Railway publicity machine to explain to the travelling public what was entailed in this new programme of works was obvious to all, and especially to Walker.

Yet it had not always been this way. The LSWR faced a similar problem when it first electrified its suburban lines in 1915/16. Desperate to win back the suburban passenger traffic which had been lost to the electric trams and Underground lines, in 1917 it released a silent film entitled *The Making of the South Western Electric*. Focussing on the speed, comfort and cleanliness of the new service as well as the new technology being employed, the film was an immediate success. Consequently, it helped the LSWR regain the business it had lost and ensured the future growth of 'the third rail'. Much of the footage was taken at the new Durnsford Road power station, Wimbledon, on the Kingston loop and at Waterloo. In 1989 the material was included in a video issued by BCL Films and retitled 'London & South Western Electric'.

The fact that the LSWR's film was such a success was a direct result of the phenomenal growth of the number of picture palaces in the early 20th century. For example, just before the outbreak of WW1 there were approximately 500 picture houses in London and its suburbs alone. Their numbers continued to grow all through the inter-war years as film-watching increased in popularity. It was pure escapism of course, but essential for many whose lives were somewhat dull and predictable.

The Southern Railway was slow to respond to the new form of entertainment and communication. Indeed, it was only after John Elliot joined Walker's staff in 1925 as Assistant for Public Relations that progress was made. As a trained journalist Elliot was fully aware of the power of positive publicity and the need to overcome the negative image of the immediate past. Thus part of Elliot's strategy was the courting of the growing British film industry which he felt had a role to play in promoting the Southern's image as a progressive, forward-looking enterprise.

The first full length feature film in which the Southern Railway actively assisted a film company was the Gainsborough Pictures production of the silent film *'The Wrecker'*. The film had a fine pedigree. It was based on the stage play co-written by Arnold Ridley and Bernard Merivale, the former subsequently achieving fame as 'Private Godfrey' in 'Dad's Army'. Michael Balcon headed Gainsborough at the time and he became a leading figure in the British film industry. Eventually he headed Ealing Studios and went on to make other railway based films such as *'The Titfield Thunderbolt'*, *'The Ladykillers'* and *'Train of Events'*. The story-line of the first of the three mentioned films also shows some similarity with *'The Wrecker'*.

'The Wrecker' was made in 1928 but not released until the following year. Made at a time of great transition in the film industry, it was one of the last silent films ever made. The stars of the film are now largely forgotten, few making it into 'the talkies' where different acting skills were needed. The story is essentially the contest between coach and train travel with the villain (Carlyle Blackwell) causing a series of train crashes on the national railway network so as to undermine public confidence. He is foiled, of course, by the heroine (Benita Hume) and the hero (Joseph Striker). The film also included that well known character, the Tart with a Heart (Pauline Johnson). Her walk is quite amazing and the film is worth watching for that alone!

The Southern Railway granted Gainsborough extensive use of its locations and facilities for the shooting of *'The Wrecker'*. These include the interior of London

Bridge signal box together with various ex SECR signal boxes. There is considerable footage of their operation. There are numerous views of Waterloo station including the station offices, the main departure board and concourse and a view through the Victory Arch to the SER Charing Cross line. Line-side locations are around Swanley and Otford with other sites on ex-SECR lines in north west Kent / south east London. The tunnel mouth sequences appear to be Penge Tunnel (the masonry work is the same) but the distances do not seem to fit. Towards the end of the film use is made of the ex-LSWR main line.

'The Wrecker' was made at a time when continuity was largely unknown. This, as far as the railway interest is concerned is its strength, for a variety of locomotive classes can be seen. From the Southern Railway's point of view pride of place was given to 'King Arthur' class No 773 *Sir Lavaine* which appears spotless. The many passing shots include L class No 756, D, L1, L11 and D15 class 4-4-0s, H15 and S15 class 4-6-0s, 700

THE WRECKER 1928. The point of impact when the F1 class 4-4-0 hits the laden Foden steam lorry on the level crossing at Lasham. Two camera towers can be seen in the foreground whilst a further camera hide is disguised as a haystack in the field just behind the rear coach. There was concern that the boiler of the steam lorry might explode when hit by a train travelling at 40 mph. Consequently these haystack hides were heavily protected with sand bags. The same crash scene was used in the 1936 film The Seven Sinners.

THE WRECKER 1928, (From left to right). The evolving scenes at Lasham on 19th August. The laden Foden steam lorry approaches the level crossing whilst the doomed 'F1' and its train approach. The locomotive falls over on its side as planned whilst the branch line's falling 1 in 50 gradient can be seen by following the line of trees. This location now forms part of the busy A339 and the railway has been totally obliterated. Escaping steam partially hides the remarkably intact derailed train. The camera hide can just be seen above the rear coaches in this and the previous scene.

and C class 0-6-0s and H16 4-6-2T. U class A803 appears throughout the film in numerous sequences. This locomotive was virtually new, having just been rebuilt from 'River' class 2-6-4T *River Itchen*. The final scene sees the hero and heroine standing on the tracks between the buffers of the 'Hopper' and the 'U' – very dramatic and romantic in 1928. Early electric units to be seen include an ex-LSWR 3-SUB unit entering Waterloo and a very brief view of the ex LBSC overhead electric just outside London Bridge. Coaching stock tends to be a mixed bag of pre-grouping types with a good sprinkling of ex-SECR Birdcage three coach sets and ex-LSWR Ironclads. Modern image enthusiasts may well drool over the new Maunsell corridor coaches.

Bus enthusiasts are not forgotten. There are shots of a fleet of London-registered Associated Daimler buses, an open-top charabanc and several 'General' NS buses with open outside stairs to the upper deck.

However, the highlight of the film was the staging of a train crash in which an express train hits a laden Foden steam lorry which has been deliberately left on a level crossing. The incident was filmed on Sunday 19th August 1928 at Salter Hatch crossing near Lasham on the little-used ex-LSWR Basingstoke to Alton branch line. Not surprisingly the event attracted considerable interest. The Southern even ran a special train from Waterloo at 3.45am so that Directors and Senior Managers could see everything. By the time it reached Basingstoke just before 5.00am the breakdown cranes and gangs from Nine Elms and Eastleigh were already in position. At the site itself, the local constabulary had to institute crowd control measures to keep the public safe and out of sight.

To ensure the crash was spectacular (which it was), the Southern prepared the groundwork in advance, after the last train had left Alton for Basingstoke the day before. Track was undermined but the formation made to look good with a series of wooden pegs and wire mesh which were covered with ballast. This ensured that the train would turn over on to its side after the crash and

would not career down the gradient towards Alton.

Gainsborough purchased the locomotive and coaches from the Southern Railway and seem to have been given a free hand as to what they did with them. The locomotive was repainted in the fictitious livery of 'United Coast Lines' at Ashford Works and moved to Lasham via Guildford. On the day, a Guildford crew manned the train. The morning was spent in rehearsals but by 1.00pm all was ready. Dummies were placed in the cab, the train was set in motion down the 1 in 50 gradient and only then did the crew jump clear. After the crash had been staged 'passengers' are seen trapped in the battered coaches and finally the rolling stock was set on fire. It was all over by about 6.00pm. The locomotive used was Stirling F1 class 4-4-0 No A148 which was specially fitted with a shortened chimney. The six coaches, the first bogie coaches designed for the SECR, had been retrieved from Streatham Hill berthing sidings.

If staging the crash had taken planning, then so did the clearing up of the debris. Immediately after filming had ceased, breakdown gangs moved in and worked all through the Sunday night removing the locomotive and the carriage under-frames from the line. The hard work paid off for the site had been cleared by the following afternoon, thus allowing the passage of the afternoon train from Basingstoke.

Gainsborough were justifiably proud of their work and wanted to make the most of the exciting sequences. Thus in *'The Wrecker'* the crash can be seen three times although from different camera angles.

So, what did the Southern Railway gain from the film, apart from getting well paid for a set of obsolete rolling stock? Primarily they were given the opportunity to show their latest locomotives and coaches together with a spacious modern terminus. Safety was a strong theme throughout the film. The core message was that the railway industry's safety measures would triumph even when faced with a criminal assault. Likewise the promotion of comfortable trains as opposed to less than

comfortable coaches was also a key feature. Throughout the film, railways are portrayed as a force for 'Good' whereas buses were the opposite; a force for 'Bad'. The fact that the villain was the railway's General Manager who consorts with a woman of dubious moral standing was probably lost on Walker. The question as to why the GM would give her a £50 note which she puts in her black stocking-top is best left unanswered!

After this obvious success, it is surprising that the Southern Railway was not used again by the film industry for some years. However, in 1936, eight years after filming 'The Wrecker', Gaumont British approached the Southern for assistance with their new film 'The Seven Sinners' starring Edmund Lowe and Constance Cummings. The story had again been written as a play by Arnold Ridley and Bernard Merivale whilst the screenplay was by Sidney Gilliatt and Frank Launder. With the same two authors it is not surprising that certain story-line similarities prevailed. This time our hero and heroine foil a group of international gun-runners whose leader covers his murderous ways by placing his victims in trains which he subsequently wrecks. How a corpse can sit in a train unnoticed is not explained; probably the villain was counting on traditional British reserve and the habit of not talking to strangers!

Many of the film's early sequences used models. but the finale needed something more realistic. Consequently Gaumont British hired a train and six coaches from the Southern Railway. The locomotive was F1 class 4-4-0 No 1060 – the same class of locomotive that was used in 'The Wrecker'. The similarities did not end there. Again the Basingstoke to Alton branch line was used for all the action shots, with the line-side sequences being taken on the 1 in 50 straight descent from the summit at Herriard. To derail the train a motor lorry was placed across the tracks and again the location chosen was Salters Hatch crossing near Lasham. The film industry, and possibly the Southern Railway, seem to have found a good site and were staying with it! The only change was the motor lorry which was a modern improvement on the steam lorry used in 1928.

The locomotive appears not to have been repainted, but all identification on the side was obliterated. There are some excellent side views of the F1 and its train. There is also a front shot of the buffer beam and smoke box, although this shot has been reversed. Nevertheless the number on the buffer beam can be seen clearly. The fact that the locomotive had been renumbered into the 1000 series shows that the film sequences were made after 1931 and not at the same time as 'The Wrecker'. However, the crash sequences were lifted straight from the 1928 film. The film industry had learnt something about continuity hence the request for the same class of locomotive. The coaches were of a different type but few would have noticed that.

All services on the Basingstoke and Alton light railway ceased on 31st May 1936 so it is likely that 'The Seven Sinners' was made after this date. This would have suited the film company who would have had the opportunity to take numerous shots and then select the best one. On the other hand the Southern Railway could have operated the train in total safety knowing that it had total line occupancy. After filming was over, and with no actual crash to clear, it is likely that lifting of the branch commenced.

The Southern Railway now had two feature film successes to its credit. Consequently it now appears that the British film industry finally recognised the positive stance of the railway company and the direct help it was prepared to give. Therefore, in 1937 only a year after

THE WRECKER 1928. Above - The Chairman of United Coast Lines railway, Sir Gervaise Bartlett (Winter Hall) has been fatally shot after suspecting who the wrecker is. 'Lucky' Roger Doyle (Joseph Striker), Mary Shelton (Benita Hume), and General Manager Ambrose Barney (Carlyle Blackwell) look on. Filmed in the offices of Waterloo station, an early photograph of a King Arthur class 4-6-0 can be seen hanging on the wall.

Left - (From top to bottom), It was a safe place for £50 in 1928! One of the may shots of 'U' class 2-6-0 No A803. 'L' class 4-4-0 on a Victoria to Ramsgate via Nunhead express races to its destruction. 3-SUB unit enters Waterloo having just completed a Kingston roundabout service.

Below - (From left to right). Benita Hume just catches one of the Southern's latest main line coaches in the chase for the Wrecker. Setting the road in an SECR signal cabin. Joseph Striker clambers over the tender to warn the locomotive crew to stop the train, a view of the 'U' class footplate taken just to the south of Otford.

Planning shunting movements in Cliddesden (Buggleskelly) station sidings in 1937. Graham Moffatt, Will Hay and Moore Marriott attempt to move some wagons so that they can access a coach for an excursion.

the filming of *'The Seven Sinners'* the Southern was approached again. This time it was Gainsborough Pictures who needed a quiet branch line and a main line station. Both had to be used for an extended period of time. The use of an operational line was totally impractical, but it so happened that the Southern had not yet finished the process of dismantling the Basingstoke to Alton branch. Lifting had commenced at the Alton end and by the time Gainsborough made their needs known demolition had reached Winslade, just to the north of Herriard. However, one country halt with its two sidings was still in situ and this, and the length of branch line remaining was just adequate for the film company's needs.

So it was that one of the classic railway films came to be filmed at Cliddesden in Hampshire. *'Oh Mr Porter!'* starring Will Hay, Moore Marriott and Graham Moffat was filmed in the summer of 1937. Based on a story by Frank Launder it is set at Buggleskelly on the Southern Railway of Northern Ireland and tells the story of how a trio of incompetents overcome a vicious gang of gun-runners. As ever, good triumphs over evil!

Not surprisingly, there is considerable footage from the Southern Railway. The credits were filmed on the LSWR main line at Popham tunnels between Basingstoke and Micheldever. Further sequences show the sharp curve leading to Southampton tunnel and the subsequent entrance to Southampton Central. The film had been reversed so that it appears that the train is running on the wrong line, but that could be excused in a Will Hay comedy!

Gainsborough completely transformed Cliddesden station. The corrugated iron station building was clad in timber, a signal box was specially built whilst a signal and a level crossing gate wheel were also additions to the site. Everything was made to look run down and neglected. Tomatoes grew in the signal box and there were marrows on the line. A haystack hid the station cottages from view. Nevertheless the station's Southern pedigree shows through the camouflage as the concrete fence posts with wire strands are quite unmistakable. In all some fifty film crew descended on Cliddesden in June 1937. This caused considerable local interest with the

BUGGLESKELLY 1937. Cliddesden station as first transformed into Buggleskelly by Gainsborough for 'Oh Mr Porter!' in 1937. The station buildings have been covered in timber whilst running in boards, signal box and signal have been specially added. Note the fictitious railway company's name, such was the attention to detail. It is not surprising that the new Station Master (Will Hay) called the station 'a dump!'. Today, the only things left on site are the horse chestnut trees, even the platform has gone.

Buggleskelly (Cliddesden) after Station Master Porter (Will Hay) decided to 'put the station on the map'. Everything has been painted, the grass has been cut and even the washing on the line has been changed! The weeds on the line seem to have had a visit from the weed killing train as well. Not surprisingly, the making of the film created considerable local interest and curious spectators look at the changes through the level crossing gates. (Author's Collection)

local paper reporting that the peaceful slumber of the village had been aroused.

Three locomotives were used for the action sequences, the main attraction being the Kent & East Sussex Railway's 2-4-0T *Northiam*. Built by Hawthorn Leslie in 1899 its works plate is clearly visible on the bunker side. For the film it was renamed 'Gladstone', the cab was cut away (so that a better view could be obtained of the actors) whilst the chimney was extended and fitted with a serrated top. The Southern Railway lent two locomotives. These were Adams X6 class 4-4-0 No 657 used for 'the express train' and Adams 395 class 0-6-0 No 3509 which was used for 'the excursion'. Both had shortened chimneys fitted whilst the Southern Railway cab-side number plates were amended with the additional wording 'of Northern Ireland' so as to fit in with the film's story line.

Gainsborough needed a tunnel for part of the story line and this was built by the studio in a cutting just to the south of Cliddesden. The final sequences have considerable footage of the branch line. It is probably true to say that these are the only moving pictures ever taken of the northern part of Britain's first authorised light railway. The line-side notices are quite distinctive whilst the SR cast iron sign has the railway company name discreetly hidden by a convenient piece of foliage.

The final action shots are taken away from the

branch. The approach to 'Belfast' is the LSWR main line between Clapham Junction and Nine Elms – I believe the third rail never made it across the Irish Sea! 'Belfast' itself was filmed in Basingstoke West goods yard. 'Gladstone' and its train had to weave through a series of placed trains and these shots are shown several times, albeit from different angles. At this point the observant will catch a glimpse of Adams O2 0-4-4T No. 200 and a passing 'Lord Nelson' on a Bournemouth West train. The Park Prewett hospital siding can also be seen climbing away in the distance. There are numerous goods vehicles to be seen in the yard including a SR meat van and several Houghton private owner wagons.

By late summer filming was complete and the lifting of the branch resumed. The film industry did not use the Southern again during the brief period of peace before WW2 started in 1939. Then the message changed entirely and focussed on enemy bomb damage and how 'the Southern could take it'. The exception was a short publicity film made in 1940. This showed the new Waterloo and City tube stock at Waterloo and included brief images of the railway's management, including Walker, Bulleid and Missenden. After nationalisation, the film industry rarely returned to the former Southern lines. Being mainly located in north and west London it is hardly surprising that the studios preferred to use lines closer to home.

Basingstoke West Yard in 1925, the final sequences in 'Oh Mr. Porter!' were filmed here. 'Gladstone' approached on the Alton branch line to the right of the hut, then swerved to its right on the long crossing thereby avoiding the Adams X6 4-4-0 stationary in its path. It then swerved back on to its original line. O2 class 0-4-4T No 200 was stationary with a train on the line to the left of the hut.

The story lines of the three feature films made on the Southern had their similarities. This was because the people who had written the original plays and screen plays were so interlinked. However, all the films have their differences. Without a doubt *'The Wrecker'* contains some of the best moving images of the early period of the Southern Railway. It is easily forgotten that at this time many Kent expresses were still being handled by 4-4-0s with only six coaches. The new moguls were few in number as were the 'King Arthurs.' By the time *'Oh Mr Porter!'* was made the railway had changed totally. With modern rolling stock and an expanding programme of electrification the Southern was a united and focussed business. Hence it could afford to laugh at itself from a position of strength. Likewise the British film industry had changed beyond recognition. The early silent era with its over-dramatic acting was long forgotten and by 1937 a high level of professionalism was evident. This can be seen by the continuity in 'Oh Mr Porter' where the staff uniforms, station name boards and the locomotives all accurately relate to the story line.

Perhaps the final words should be taken from the Southern Railway magazine. In one of its 1937 editions it stated that 'Cliddesden's challenge to Hollywood is no more'. On the front page it had a portrait of Sir Herbert Walker announcing his retirement as General Manager. Certainly the articles were fitting memorials to a unique period in Southern Railway history.

With special thanks to Bob Geoghegan of The Archive Film Agency for his assistance and for the fact that he rekindled my interest in old British films.

CLAPHAM JUNCTION SIGNALLING SCHOOL

Above and page 32 - Three views of the Southern Railway and later Southern Region signal school at Clapham Junction, located on the footbridge but subsequently destroyed by fire. (A fire in the buildings and footbridge is known to have occurred in 1981, but was there an earlier one as well?)

Save what can be gleaned from the actual views, nothing is known of this remarkable installation, which when photographed, was in pristine condition. How much use it had and its origins are also unknown although there is perhaps a hint of pre-SR about it - why not, the LBSCR were reported to have had their own training school.

Much of the equipment would appear to be current SR or BR(S) type, whilst the scale, at a guess, might well be 'Gauge 1'. What a wonderful rendition also of a contemporary Southern EMU motor–coach: there were at least two, as well as two large tank engines in a distinctive 'Brighton' style. Notice in the distance the various types of single line instruments as well.

Somewhat prophetic is the notice in the left background, 'Emergency Exit Hatch in Case of Fire'.

Any further information would be welcome.

Just as we were going to print with this issue a further view arrived plus information on the earlier LSWR signal school at Wimbledon. More then for the future!

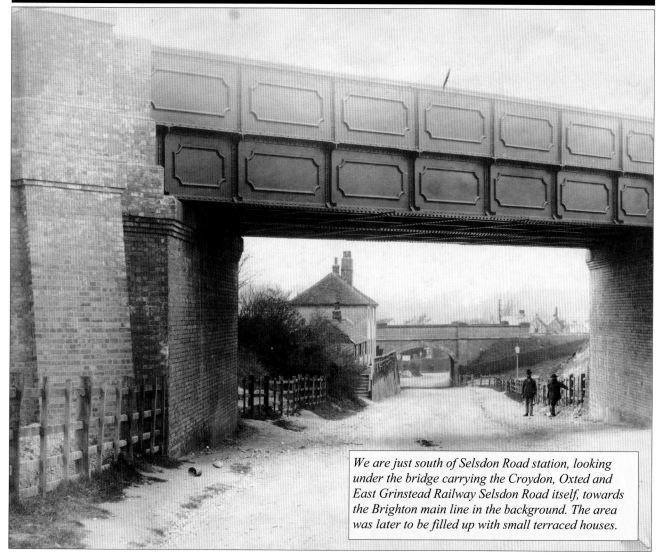

We are just south of Selsdon Road station, looking under the bridge carrying the Croydon, Oxted and East Grinstead Railway Selsdon Road itself, towards the Brighton main line in the background. The area was later to be filled up with small terraced houses.

These photographs were taken immediately after completion of the Croydon, Oxted & East Grinstead Railway in 1884, probably for the contractor, Joseph Firbank, and are reproduced from original contact prints made from the glass plates. A few have been copied over the years but this is the first time that most of them have been reproduced. They are of great value in showing a range of bridges and other structures when new before they were partly obscured by vegetation. There are also views of Upper Warlingham and Oxted stations, taken as part of the same series, copies of which are in the Lens of Sutton Collection, but these were not among the original prints seen here. Similar sets of views were made of the Chichester-Midhurst line and that between Oxted and Ashurst.

The Selsdon-East Grinstead line involved some heavy works, cutting as it did through the North Downs and the High Weald near East Grinstead. The section seen in the initial set of views made use of the abandoned Surrey & Sussex Junction line of the 1860s but there is nothing visible in them to indicate that the works were not completely new. The engineering works on the line as a whole included three substantial viaducts of wrought iron girders at Riddlesdown, Oxted and Cook's Pond, together with a great many lesser brick and iron bridges.

Notes by John Minnis

Sanderstead station looking northwards. The timber footbridge, replaced in later pre-grouping days is prominent, as are the station awnings. Although some writers have suggested that the stations were built to South Eastern Railway designs, they have much in common with LB&SCR timber stations of the period, especially as regards the shape of the awnings and valancing style (e.g. Hampden Park and Fittleworth). Following destruction by fire in 1986, the station was completely rebuilt in the pleasing style favoured by BR at the time.

An underbridge near Sanderstead.

Looking along the line near Sanderstead with a Saxby & Farmer distant signal in the background

The south portal of the 836 yard long Riddlesdown Tunnel, giving an idea of the extent of the works needed to build the line. A station was opened in 1927 a little to the north of the tunnel.

Riddlesdown Viaduct, looking north, similar in form to the other two major viaducts on the line with its brick piers and riveted lattice girders. Additional strengthening piers were added by the 1900s .

A companion view of Riddlesdown Viaduct looking south, showing its spectacular setting with the lime works below.

An iron lattice girder footbridge spanning the line a little to the south of Upper Warlingham station.

All from the RCHS / Spence Collection

A further selection will appear in a future issue.

With thanks to Clive Warneford who submitted the illustration.

CLAPHAM JUNCTION
10th May1965

It would be tempting to start this piece with all sorts of obvious quips similar to, 'Chaos at Clapham' or even 'Did you feel the earth move?', instead it may be more appropriate to confine ourselves to the facts of what is still a well-remembered incident although one where the conclusions may be perhaps less known.

Clapham Junction 'A' Box dated from around 1905 and comprised two 120 feet steel girders spanning some eleven sets of rails. These were the four Windsor lines, two Kensington lines and three sidings. The actual box structure contained an electric power frame of 103 levers placed parallel to the running lines. At the time of the incident the box was dealing with around 1,250 train movements daily. Simply put, there were four corner points of contact supporting the box and it was an end diagonal near the north-west corner, which failed without warning at 8.36 am, on Monday 10th May 1965.

As might be expected, the whole incident could not have occurred at a worst time, at the height of the morning rush-hour. The signalmen on duty were alerted to the developing situation by the noise of the falling girder and the fact their working environment was rapidly assuming a drunken angle. It must have been a frightening experience, but nevertheless they placed all signals at danger and sent the emergency code of six bells 'obstruction danger', before evacuating the box. It was only when outside that the full extend of the situation became clear and which is apparent from the photographs. The effect on train services was understandably profound.

Attached to the structure, but at the end furthest away from where the failure had occurred, was a signal gantry spanning the Up and Down Main through and local lines. It was quickly established that this gantry had not been affected and for a while trains were allowed to pass underneath at restricted speed. Fear though that vibration might cause the failed girder to collapse, resulted in these movements being stopped shortly afterwards.

Meanwhile in an attempt to afford some sort of service to passengers whose intended destination was Waterloo, up line services were halted at Wimbledon with passengers diverted to either the central section or London Transport. Steam services which had not yet reached Woking were terminated there, although boat trains from Southampton were diverted to arrive at Victoria. An electric shuttle service was later initiated between Wimbledon and Clapham Junction and also between Barnes and Clapham Junction, services from Windsor, Richmond, Reading and Hounslow etc, being terminated at Barnes.

It had been hoped that sufficient repairs might be completed to allow a close to normal evening return service from Waterloo, but these could not be finished in time and instead arrangements were made to commence main line Bournemouth services from Woking. It was a credit to the operational side of the Southern that the evening services ran smoothly albeit with far longer journey times. Interestingly, no mention is made of the disruption to services, ECS or otherwise, which had already left Waterloo that morning.

As an emergency measure, the 75ton Nine Elms breakdown crane was despatched to support the fallen girder. Steel trestles were then built up from ground level under the damaged girder itself which was in turn slowly raised by jacks. Fortunately the weather was favourable and less than 24 hours after the occurrence all lines, excepting the up Windsor local, were reopened for traffic although again to reduce vibration, at restricted speed. By the evening of 11th May, the up Windsor local was also open and speed restrictions were removed a week later.

At the time, Southern Region instructions were that structures of this type should be inspected every two years, the last of these being on 3rd May 1964, when Examiner W Shelley commented on heavy corrosion but without reference to a failed diagonal member. This had been noted previously in 1961. The 1964 report was passed to and indeed initialled by the Divisional Engineer, Mr R A Hammet, although it subsequently transpired he had not seen the vital earlier report of February 1961 in which a number of items were marked for attention.

Unfortunately a lack of communication, pressure of work elsewhere and poor co-ordination between departments had allowed what was a serious situation to worsen. The priority at that time was to inspect other structures considered to be under greater stress. Even so no one person could be held responsible, it was the fault of the 'system', a point made by the Inspecting Officer, Col.

Opposite - *An unidentified 'T9' approaching Clapham Junction with a Waterloo - Southampton Terminus working. 'A' Box is in the background minus its protective metal covering which was added in late 1940. In the background is the carriage wash.* Ian Pope collection.

Above - *Monday afternoon and the Nine Elms crane is being prepared to attach lifting chains to prevent any further collapse. Two men can also be seen on the structure itself.*

Left - 35001 'Channel Packet' heads through Clapham junction with the down 'Devon Belle' in September 1950.
Right - Complete, on 13th July 1954. It will be noted that the wartime roof covering is still present. This was subsequently removed to save weight following the 1965 collapse although the supporting skeletal frame remained until the end.

The morning of 10th May, prior to the arrival of the Nine Elms crane. The power frame of 103 levers had been installed in 1936, operating colour light signals and electric point motors. The structure fell some four feet at the time of the collapse, not helped by the additional loading caused by the wartime roof. This roof covering alone was estimated to weight 30 tons and brought the weight of the whole structure to an estimated 200 tons.

D McMullen. He was also scathing in his comments over the catastrophe that might have resulted had a total collapse occurred when a train was passing underneath, citing the Lewisham disaster as an example. Indeed Col. McMullen had every reason to be scathing, as in June 1963 a signal gantry had collapsed at Ferryhill on the North Eastern Region for similar reasons, but the resulting report was not subsequently circulated to the other BR regions.

Now though it was different. As a direct result of the Clapham Junction collapse, new procedures were put in place and a reorganisation took place of what was the Woking Civil Engineers District. What was at once apparent was that other similar structures might equally be at risk and an immediate examination of the nearby West London Junction signalbox revealed a risk of similar failure likely.

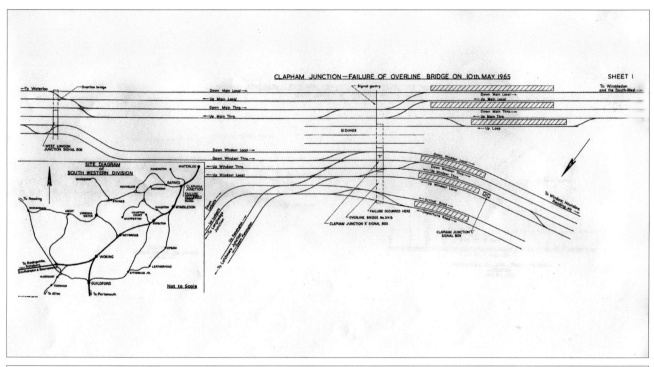

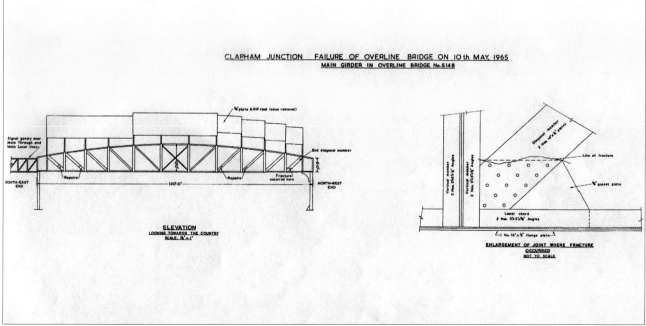

Location map and bridge repair history, taken from the inspecting officer's report.

This page, 11th May 1965, the day after the collapse and the trestling referred to can be seen in place. The 'Railway Observer' covered the story as under in the July issue, "....all traffic in and out of Waterloo came to a halt, with stationary trains standing at every signal far out into the suburbs. Most of the morning was occupied in detraining passengers, in some cases between stations, and getting things moving again. Even during the early afternoon a large proportion of incoming trains was being turned back at Surbiton. At about two o'clock a down Bournemouth express which had been extricated from the jam left Surbiton behind 34006 running tender-first. For the evening rush-hour period Wimbledon became the terminus for electric trains on the Portsmouth, Guildford and Epsom lines, while Barnes and Twickenham were the starting points for the Windsor Line. The Kingston Roundabout service ran spasmodically to and from Clapham Junction using the up local line from Earlsfield as a single line to reach the station from the Wimbledon direction. Shuttle services operated on the suburban branches, and a special nonstop service was run between Victoria and Wimbledon via Tooting. Steam services mainly terminated at Woking and engines were turned on the Addlestone triangle. However, the 17.43 Waterloo-Salisbury departed from the up local platform at Surbiton, with 73080 on the stock off an up morning train which had terminated there. Later in the evening D805 arrived at Surbiton with the empty carriages of the 14.20 from Exeter, followed by 34084 on a Bournemouth train's stock, and both trains were berthed for the night. The overnight mail and newspaper trains started from either Victoria or Paddington, and during the day up boat trains had been diverted to Victoria. Emergency repairs to the gantry were completed in time for Tuesday's traffic to reach Waterloo except for some cancellations on the Windsor line. However, rolling stock was scattered far and wide, the 08.30 to Bournemouth was formed almost entirely of first-class coaches from a boat train set, and incoming Basingstoke trains provided the stock for the 08.35 and 09.00. The evening rush-hour traffic was badly delayed by the speed restriction through Clapham Junction, and by disrupted carriage rosters. Many rush-hour electrics had only four cars, and one up Reading train approaching Waterloo about six o'clock was formed of two cars only. The trestles which now support the buckled gantry have blocked the access to the West London platforms, numbers 1 and 2, and the Kensington Olympia trains now use the Central Section platforms." At this point the story of Clapham in the 'R.O'" ended, but on the basis that trouble rarely comes alone, this is what followed; "After two days of normality at Waterloo, Friday the 14th brought a temperature of 82 degrees which caused a conductor rail on the up through line at Vauxhall to buckle in the middle of the evening rush-hour, resulting in more queues of stationary trains. During the morning rush-hour, up trains

were delayed when the 07.30 Basingstoke-Waterloo stopped at Berrylands when the right hand side cab sheet of 34024 came away. Some vigorous hammering by the fireman righted matters enough to get the train to Waterloo fifteen minutes late."

The inspecting officers report also questioned the practicalities of the previous inspections, several having had to be carried out with a torch at night. It was certainly never admitted that pressure to release the lines to traffic meant daytime inspections were discouraged. Clapham Junction 'A' was also affected by fires in 1980, 1985 and finally 1986, the last serious enough to require complete rewiring. Two years later in 1988, a fault in the wiring of the associated relay room led to the 1988 Clapham accident.

Below - And all the time the rot was slowly taking place; 'M7' No 30249 shunting milk tanks destined for Kensington Olympia at Clapham, Sunday 26th April 1963. During the course of the disruption, Kensington trains were rerouted into Platforms 16 and 17.   Lens of Sutton collection.

Late LSWR to early BR
(with a few gaps in-between)
James Eltham

A chance conversation and a new friend to *Southern Way*. James Eltham's late father was an enthusiast all his life, fortunately recording the railway scene along the way, a facet followed by James as well. Whilst not in any way pretending these are all of the best quality, they are nevertheless fascinating, certainly never seen before and record the transition from Drummond to Urie including the rebuilding of the various Drummond double-singles. Later we progress through the early days of BR, times of mixed liveries and just a hint of the first of the Standard classes on the way.

A unique and very personal collection, a gem of a result and concluded with a wonderful tribute from a son to his father. "My poor father really had no chance. Born to a mother who thought it a good idea to take her son to see the 'Great Bear' and educated at Colet Court prep. school prior to St. Paul's, the G.W.R. was his first love. After wartime RAF service and becoming Poole Pottery's works manager, it was the Southern's turn, with a smattering of S and D. Befriending loco driver Bill Dodge, footplate trips in the Poole area ensued, my father using the whistle to signal to mother his imminent return home.

"At all times during his life, father meticulously noted and photographed the workings and when living in Woking, I also well recall the sacked and bound nameplates which Eastleigh and Swindon occasionally delivered to the door. '*Lord Howe*', '*Sir Prianius*', '*Stephenson*', '*Glastonbury Abbey*' and '*Penrice Castle*' were amongst those collected for their love - and later sold, before any price boom!

"Father made sure that he, my brother and I would be at Woking station to see the rebuilt 35018 on its inaugural run and the sight of what surely was the most handsome pacific ever created will never be forgotten.

"His older friend, Brian Cannon, was a suitable railway collaborator and a correspondence with Hamilton Ellis was enjoyed over a long period.

"The demise of steam never dampened father's interest and being a true progressive, he responded with enthusiasm to the modern age, never hankering for bygone sights, unlike his younger son!"

Left *- Byfleet, circa 1925. The relief portion of the 9.30 am Waterloo to Bournemouth service is passing the station behind 'L12' No 421. This was the engine in charge of the passenger service from Plymouth involved in the Salisbury disaster of June 1906. Completed at Nine Elms in September 1904, it remained in service for 47 years being withdrawn in September 1951.*

Bottom *- Approaching Woking from Portsmouth, is 'S11' 4-4-0 No 399. This was the first of the 10 engines in the class to be fitted with an 'Eastleigh' pattern superheated, extended smokebox and new chimney in May 1920. This modification made the type suitable for Portsmouth line workings although they were later replaced by D15s, in turn superseded on the Bournemouth line by the new 'King Arthur' type. No 399 was subsequently at Exmouth Junction and Bournemouth. During WW2 the entire class were transferred to the LMS for service on the S & D but were also seen further afield. No 399 returned to the SR at Bournemouth in 1945. The final shed for30399 became Fratton with some of its last duties between Reading and Redhill. The engine lasted until December 1951.*

Drummond 'G14' 4-6-0 No 456 at Byfleet possibly in its last days of service. Built at Nine Elms in May 1908, Bradley refers to No 456 as the only member of the five in the class to have been fitted with a non-water-tube firebox, although the photograph would tend to imply otherwise. As is well known, along with most of the Drummond 4-6-0 types, the class was not considered worth retaining long term and all five were laid aside in January 1925 although their tenders were re-used.

'H15' 4-6-0 No 488 approaching Woking with a Basingstoke to Waterloo service. This was another engine to have been involved in an accident, this time when just seven months old, in October 1914 at Andover Junction. The loco was in charge of a forty wagon train and ran into the rear of a stationary Yeovil - Nine Elms goods. Such was the force of the impact that the engine ploughed into some 20 vehicles of the stationary service before it came to rest, its own train piled up behind. Years later the fireman remarked how he recalled , "... the sight of a fully loaded cattle wagon sliding along the boiler and being flung through the air to land on the rear van of the train standing in the Swindon (MSWJ) bay." Members of the class worked both freight and passenger services. No 30488 was withdrawn in 1959 and the last members of the class went in 1961.

Sometime between November 1918 and August 1920, R.O.D No 2122 heads an up goods through Byfleet. This was one of 17 of the type loaned / hired to the LSWR at intervals during this period. No 2122 is previously thought to have worked mainly between Exmouth Junction and Salisbury. No 2122 subsequently went to the GWR as their No 3053. It remained in service until February 1929.

Left - *Another superheated 'S11', this time No 396 entering Byfleet with the 7.40 am Salisbury to Waterloo. As referred to on the previous page, the class were transferred to the LMS for S & D duties during the 1940s which included No 396 piloting the S & D 2-8-0 type on heavy coal trains. Later, in 1944, this engine was repaired at Derby. As No 30396, it was the first of the class to receive BR black livery, not all the type being repainted before withdrawal. Despite a fresh external appearance the mechanical condition by that time was poor and No 30396 was withdrawn in December 1951.*

End of the line for four Drummond 4-6-0's, three of which are recorded as 'G14's 455, 451 and 456, seen at Eastleigh on 29th April 1925. Of these, No 451 at least had been laid aside as unserviceable on 23/12/1924, whilst No 455 had been repainted in Maunsell green and renumbered E455. On paper at least they were rebuilt as 'King Arthur' 4-6-0s although little except the tenders was actually reused.

Following a successful trial on the Isle of Wight lines of Nos 206 and 211 in May 1923, two further members of the 'O2' class, Nos 205 and 215, were shipped in pieces from mainland Hampshire to St Helens Wharf / Quay in June 1924 and reassembled at Ryde by fitters sent across from Eastleigh. Renumbered for Isle of Wight use as No 21, the former LSWR No 205 was subsequently given the name 'Sandown'. It would remain in service on the Island lines for a further 40 years being one of the last to be withdrawn in May 1966, more than 30 years after the first of the mainland 'O2s has ceased working. No 21 is pictured at the front of Eastleigh Works yard on 15th April 1924, fully two months before transfer.

The view was taken from the steps on the corner of Campbell Road, at the point where the road makes a 90° turn having crossed the Southampton running lines and running shed access roads. From this point, a wide set of steps led down to ground level at what was known as No 1 gate, obviously used solely by pedestrians. Gate 2, approximately 100 yards to the right was the first that might be used by wheeled vehicles. Even so it was not uncommon to see bicycles being carried up and down these steps. To the right is the timekeeper's office which also served as a security gate, each of the formal access points being watched in this way. On the left is the corner of the main office block, with the actual works buildings out of camera to the right. Shift changeover times would witness hundreds of men ascending or descending the steps accordingly.

In the background, the wagons are standing in what was referred to as Tipton Yard, which ran from the station, out of camera to the left and alongside the Fareham and Gosport line, which is itself between the works yard and aforementioned sidings. Rail access to the works was via a metal gate and single siding running in front of the office block which in turn connected into the shed access lines from the running line. The carriage works was on the opposite side of the complex behind the sidings and ran basically in a north to south direction.

Top left - *The first day of service for the new 'Royal Wessex' service, Thursday 3rd May 1951. The Weymouth portion is seen here behind 34105 'Swanage', attached to two SR corridor thirds and a five coach set of Mk1 vehicles. All in the latest 'blood and custard' livery - referred to by John Elliot as 'raspberries and cream'. This first service left Weymouth at 7.38 am and despite a bout of slipping in Bincombe Tunnel was reported as almost right time at Waterloo. Six additional vehicles were added at Bournemouth, the 13 coach train, equal to 446 tons, a severe test for a 'West Country'.*

Centre left - *A continental special working from Victoria on 5th April 1951 with 34071 '601 Squadron' in charge. To the right is the tender of 30764 'Sir Gawain'.*

Below - *70009 'Alfred the Great' at Bournemouth Central on 7th June 1951, waiting to leave for Waterloo. This was one of two 'Britannia' pacifics then based at Nine Elms, the other was No 70014. At the same time Nine Elms had lost 34039, 34057 and 34065 on loan to the Eastern Region. At this stage No 70009 was mainly working the 8.30 from Waterloo and 1.05 return, but the type subsequently also hauled the 'Bournemouth Belle' as well as a Waterloo - Exeter service.*

Above *- Five and bit months into nationalisation and the signs are beginning to show. Renumbered No 30700 sandwiched between No 860 'Lord Hawke' and 791 'Sir Uwaine'.*

Centre *- At intervals between November 1951 and November 1952, ten members of the 4-4-0 'L' class were transferred to Eastleigh working light passenger trains in lieu of withdrawn Drummond 4-4-0s. Mostly they stayed around the central Hampshire area including taking fruit trains from Swanwick although here a clean No 31770 is recorded at Bournemouth shed on 9th February 1952.*

Right *- On 8th April 1950, 'M7' No 30106 comes off the line from Broadstone with a Brockenhurst - Bournemouth service, via Wimborne. On paper this engine was withdrawn in November 1960 although in practice it would swap identities with No 30667 in March 1961 and survived at work as one of the last members of the class until May 1964.*

Eastleigh, 4ᵗʰ March 1950. Of the three engines seen in the two views, one, No 30850 survives, the other two, 'L11' No 413 and 'O2' No 30225 long being recycled into a new guise.

Above - On the same date, 30451 'Sir Lamorak' was fresh from overhaul and transferred to the running shed before return to its home depot of Basingstoke. Below - On an unreported date although likely to be the summer of 1949, 'H2' No 32421 'South Foreland' has emerged from the confines of Eastleigh Works and stands resplendent in fresh black livery although the tender crest is still awaited.

Above - 'T14' 4-6-0 No 444 out of use and recently withdrawn from Eastleigh. Two of the class, this machine and No 462 were withdrawn in February 1950, leaving just two in service. The last, No 461 went in June 1951.
Below - 30757 'Earl of Mount Edgcumbe' on the occasion of an Eastleigh RCTS visit, possibly around the same time.

Page 57, top and opposite page top - *30747 'Elaine' fresh from overhaul on and ready for traffic. Well almost, as it was noted by the photographer that the bolts securing the chimney appeared not to have been fully fitted home.*

Page 57, middle - *At the same time, 'G16' 4-8-0 No 30493 had been similarly outshopped. Noted behind was 'Schools' No 914 'Eastbourne' and 'B4' No 94.*

Page 57, bottom - *Still on the books so to speak, but clearly in store, 'T9' No 30300 is in reasonable external condition but with the tell-tale sacking over the chimney. Waiting perhaps for the start of the summer service? 20th May 1950.*

Opposite page, bottom - *'Terrier' No 13, formerly part of the IOW number series but transferred back to the mainland and renumbered as BR No 32677 in August 1949. The view was taken on 14th May 1949. Alongside is another IOW engine, the former No 8 'Freshwater', which was renumbered as 32646 at the same time.*

This page, top - *'L11' No 30175 seemingly out of use at Eastleigh on 20th May 1950. In fact the engine would have a further lease of life on local services around the area which included a van train to Bournemouth in October 1951 after which it ventured on to the Somerset & Dorset route as far as Bath. This was however a swansong, for it was withdrawn the following month.*

This page, bottom - *'J1' 4-6-2T No 32325 and 'I3' 4-4-2T No 32086 outside Brighton. Both would see limited service under BR being retired in June 1951 and October 1951 respectively.*

SCUPPERING THE "U-BOATS"

Following dieselisation of the Redhill - Reading line in January 1965 it looked as if time was up for Maunsell's 'U' and 'N' Class Moguls. Remarkably they managed to survive in service for another eighteen months as *Jeffery Grayer* recalls.

The final quartet of Maunsell moguls, comprising two 'U' Class and two 'N' Class, remaining in service on the Southern Region of British Railways were withdrawn from Guildford shed in June 1966, just over a year before the end of steam on the region in July 1967. That these designs should have lasted in service for nearly 40 years in the case of the 'U's, having been introduced in 1928, and for nearly 50 years in the case of the 'N's, having been introduced in 1917, is a testament to their durability and usefulness in service where they became known as the Region's "maids of all work" equally at home on both passenger and freight workings. 60 'U' Class were built, including 20 rebuilds from River class 2-6-4Ts, the first withdrawal, 31630, not occurring until November 1962. 80 N Class were built with the first withdrawals, 31409 / 31414, also coming in November 1962.

We take up the story in early 1965 when, as Appendix 1 illustrates, there were just 10 examples of Class 'U' and 12 of Class 'N' on the books, formerly allocated to both Redhill and Guildford sheds but in January all were concentrated at 70C with the closure of 75B which became a maintenance depot. On 4th January steam's reign on the Tonbridge – Reading line had come to an end with dieselisation and to most enthusiasts' ears this effectively sounded the death knell for the future of these moguls even though it was anticipated that a few would probably continue to undertake a number of parcels workings on this line and be called upon to substitute for the inevitable failures of diesels on passenger services. For the record, locomotives noted at work on the last day of steam services included 31620 / 31627 / 31816 / 31401 / 31842 and 31831 with 31411 working an LCGB special from Redhill to Tonbridge. Surprisingly mass withdrawal did not immediately follow dieselisation and a variety of work was somehow found for them which was to prolong their life for another eighteen months.

Examples of such regular passenger steam duties to be taken on by the moguls were the 0732 and 0845 Woking – Basingstoke stopping trains. The locomotive from the 0732 later worked to Southampton Terminus taking on the 1610 to Bournemouth Central and returning at 1840 to Woking, Performers on these duties in February 1965 included 31408 / 31639 / 31803 / 31809 / 31866.

February also saw moguls on Basingstoke – Nine Elms freight turns, 31803 appearing on 6th of the month with 31619 showing up on the 11th. For a considerable period 31405 was to find work on the 0756 Three Bridges – Eastbourne goods followed by Bexhill – Lewes and Lewes -Three Bridges freight turns. The Guildford moguls also obtained employment in the London area with 31619 seen shunting at Surbiton on 9th February, the same day that 31803 was at Wimbledon West Yard having worked one of the Chessington branch coal trains. The Morden South – Clapham Junction milk trains and, further afield, the Salisbury-Portsmouth van trains also witnessed mogul haulage at this time and 31619 even tackled a 19 vehicle parcels train from Waterloo on the 19th February.

February 22nd saw them take over the 0700 Reading – Southampton Terminus working and in March a down freight to Eastleigh had 31803 at its head. On 16th March 31842 worked two AC electric sets over from Ilford to Eastleigh for overhaul. June saw a number of moguls recorded on various freight workings supplemented by 31401's appearance on the 1430 Weymouth-Eastleigh passenger turn. Until the end of the 1965/66 winter timetable the 1840 Bournemouth West-Woking often played host to moguls including 31800, 31619 and 31639. 31791 made several appearances during May on the morning goods from Three Bridges-Eastbourne but by the end of the month diesel haulage was becoming more prevalent. 31811 took the 1800 from Eastbourne to Tunbridge Wells West on 20th May and the 0736 from Eastbourne on the 28th May. The 9th saw 31809 at Nine Elms rostered for the following day's 0600 freight departure for Wimbledon. Late July saw a shortage of Type 3 diesels to work the busy 1708 Reading – Redhill service and Standard and Maunsell mogul power again came to the rescue on their former stamping ground. October 9th saw 31408 at Wimbledon on the up slow line with a parcels train which was the usual preserve of Standard motive power

In connection with the forthcoming Bournemouth electrification, work was progressing, during November 1965, with the laying of continuous welded rails on the down and up through lines between Winchfield and Farnborough and it became common to see surviving

*Opposite page - Happier times for members of the 'U' and 'N' classes. Top - 'U' 31627 and another unidentified mogul, doublehead down the bank to Gomshall with a westbound train to Reading, 18th April 1958. This particular engine survived until October 1965 having had a working life of 36½ years. **Bottom** - 'N' 31855 at London Bridge ready to work the 1.25 pm Brighton, via East Grinstead, service in September 1953. Built in 1925 it lasted until December 1964 having been fitted with new frames in 1955. At the time is was photographed, this was a Bricklayers Arms engine.*

members of U and N Class at work on ballast trains here. Further work provided for them was on additional Reading parcels trains prior to Christmas 1965, and on Woking – New Cross Gate ballast trains which they handled along with Standard classes, their final workings on the SR's Central Section involving 31803 on 10th February 1966 and 31639 on 21st April.

10th January 1966 saw 31411 at Hook with the 0732 Woking – Basingstoke and in the station on a stone train was 31803 whilst on the same day 31408 was noted at Winchfield on a ballast cleaner train. On the 7th. January 31806 worked the 1906 Portsmouth – Eastleigh vans and Ns were noted as regular performers on Waterloo ecs duties. Following the withdrawals of January, only six moguls now remained in stock and on the 23rd. January 31411, 31639, 31791, 31873 were all noted on Guildford shed but they could still be seen out on the road on ballast trains between Hook and Basingstoke. On the 23rd. January 31866 was seen undergoing attention at Nine Elms with a detached tender only to be withdrawn later the same month. As the likely withdrawal of the remaining members edged ever closer they became increasingly popular motive power for railtours such as that run on the 20th. March when 31639 worked the RCTS Solent Railtour together with 75070. The day before it had been seen on the 0732 Woking – Basingstoke and later the same day on the 1146 Eastleigh – Southampton Terminus eight coach ecs train, subsequently returning to Eastleigh for servicing. Appendix 2 details the railtours on which moguls performed in 1965/66. All the moguls on these specials performed so competently that it was difficult to believe that their long innings was coming to a close.

On 20th. March 31405 / 31408 were both on ballast trains at Woking and although the 0732 Woking –

Basingstoke was still diagrammed for a mogul, in practice a Standard Class 5 was usually to be found working it. This was probably the only passenger train at that time diagrammed for a Maunsell mogul. The return working for this duty was now the 0921 Basingstoke to Guildford shed light engine. The end finally came in June 1966 when the last quartet was withdrawn. Their work had been taken over by Standard Class 4 2-6-0s and by the interloper 77014 which had been surprisingly transferred in from the Midland Region in June 1965 following arrival on the SR on a goods service from its home depot of Northwich (9C) in March. Apparently the shed staff at Guildford were sorry to see the moguls go as they had always been popular engines requiring a lot less maintenance work than some of the other types to keep them running. The condition of many of the survivors was a testament to the affection in which they were held by shed staff. David Shepherd visited the shed on many occasions and recorded one of the moguls for posterity in one of his many railway paintings.

The last two moguls to remain at Guildford shed were 31408 and 31639 which were noted on shed with their motion dismantled awaiting disposal in late June and they, together with 73170, were towed from Guildford to Eastleigh on July 1st by 73082 'Camelot'. Thus ended the long association of Guildford shed and Maunsell moguls which stretched back some 40 years to the 1920s when they had first been allocated there. At Eastleigh shed on 3 July the last mogul survivors, newly arrived from Guildford, joined their classmates 31411 and 31803 which had been withdrawn back in April. During the week of 20th. August the moguls left Eastleigh for their appointment with the South Wales scrap dealers. Fortunately three Us and one N, which had been

Opposite page - 'N' class No 31866 at on the turntable at Guildford, 27th July 1965. This was one of the final twelve active members of the class all of which were then concentrated at Guildford and Redhill, but as their former locomotive-hauled workings on the Reading - Redhill line were slowly given over to diesel traction so the remaining engines were seen further afield often on engineers workings.

Above - 'U' No 31809 and 'N' 31842 looking into the rear of Guildford shed, 27th July 1965. Both were taken out of service within the next six months.   *Pete Moody*

Right - 31411 (in company with 31803), at Forest Row on 13th June 1965 with the LCGB 'Wealdsman' railtour.

withdrawn back in 1964, were destined for Woodham's yard at Barry and ultimate preservation although a couple had to spend some 16 years waiting for eventual rescue.

Five of the Mogul type escaped the cutters torch , 31618 (U), withdrawn January 1964, mileage 1,143,942. Stored initially at Fratton before moving to Woodhams Yard under its own steam, towing 31638, in June 1964. Purchased January 1969 for £2,000 by the Southern Mogul Preservation Society. Based initially at New Hythe, then moved to the KESR and finally to the Bluebell Railway where the Maunsell Locomotive Society is now the owner.

31806 (U) withdrawn January 1964, mileage 1,099,647. Purchased October 1976 and moved to the Mid Hants Railway.

31625 (U), withdrawn January 1964. Purchased March 1980 and moved to the Mid Hants Railway.

31638 (U), withdrawn January 1964. Purchased July 1980 by the Bluebell Railway, now has an ex-Schools Class tender fitted.

31874 (N), withdrawn March 1964. Purchased March 1974 and moved to Mid Hants Railway where it hauled the re-opening train on 30th April 1977.

One of the what were destined to be last of the four active moguls, 'U' No 31639 seen at Eastleigh on 19th March 1966, the others were 'U' 31791, and 'N's 31869 and 31872 all of which were withdrawn in June 1966.   *Pete Moody*

Appendix 1 - Withdrawal of Maunsell Moguls January 1965 - June 1966		
'U' Class	**Withdrawn**	**'N' Class**
31799 b	February 1965	
31620 n	April 1965	31831 n 31862 n
31790 n	May 1965	
	July 1965	31401 n 31811 b
	September 1965	31842 n
31627 n 31800 n	October 1965	
31619 c	December 1965	31858 b
31809 c	January 1966	31866 c 31816 n 31873 n
31803 n	March 1966	
	April 1966	31411 n
31639 n 31791 n	June 1966	31405 n 31408 n
Notes: -	n - Scrapped at Cashmore's, Newport c - Scrapped by Cohen's Kettering, but cut up on site at Eastleigh b - Scrapped at Buttigieg's, Newport	

Appendix 2 - Mogul operated Railtours June 1965 - June 1966			
Loco	**Tour**	**Date**	**Route**
31803 / 31411	LCGB Wealdsman	13th June 1965	Three Bridges - Heathfield - Hastings - Eastbourne - Haywards Heath
31866	LCGB Steyning Line	5th December 1965	Waterloo - Horsham - Steyning - Brighton - Steyning - Sutton - Streatham
31639	RCTS Somerset & Dorset	2nd January 1966	Broadstone - Bath Green Park (with 34105)
31639	LCGB S15 Commemorative No 1	9th January 1966	Bordon Branch
31639	LCGB S15 Commemorative No 2	16th January 1966	Bordon Branch
31411	SCTS Southdown Venturer	20th February 1966	Fareham - Gosport - Portsmouth Harbour
31639	RCTS Solent	20th March 1966	Gosport Branch. Fareham - Guildford - East Putney - Waterloo (with 75070)
31639 / 31411	LCGB Wilts and Hants	3rd April 1966	Waterloo - Twickenham - Clapham Junction - Crystal Palace - East Croydon - Redhill - Basingstoke - Salisbury - Southampton - Alton - Waterloo (with 33006)
31639 / 31411	RCTS Longmoor No 1	16th April 1966	Waterloo - Woking - Liss - Bordon - Staines - Windsor - Waterloo
31639 / 31411	RCTS Longmoor No 2	30th April 1966	Waterloo - Woking - Liss - Bordon - Staines - Windsor - Waterloo

SCUPPERING THE "U-BOATS" - YEARS EARLIER

As is known, the 'U' class were a direct descendent of the ill fated 'River' class 2-6-4T design, rebuilt as 2-6-0 tender engines following the 1927 Sevonoaks disaster.

Save for one well-known view showing the locomotive involved, No A800 'River Cray', resting against the cutting side subsequent to the accident, few photographs of the engine in the immediate aftermath have been located - until now.

Above - No 790 the first of the class dating from July 1917 and named 'River Avon' in January 1925.

Left - The nearside of No A800 after removal to Ashford. At the time the engine was just 13 months old. In this view the damage shown was relatively minor, dented and damaged plating consistent with a side scrape against the cutting side and overbridge. More serious of course, was that seen on the opposite page.

With grateful thanks to Mike Roberts for the loan of the three Ashford views.
Payment for this article has been made to the PHYLLIS TUCKWELL HOSPICE at Farnham.

'*Outside the greasehouse at Ashford Works before the engine was sheeted over*'. *Despite the poor conditions for photography, the views here tell a different story. Missing completely is the front Bissel truck, the left hand wheel from which had become dislodged and was subsequently found minus three spokes. Equally serious is the totally missing left hand cylinder, swiped off as the engine rolled left through the brick overbridge. It was this bridge which was responsible for much of the damage to the following rolling stock and consequent fatalities. Little mention of this damage is made in the Inspecting officer's report, the missing wheel certainly a consequence of the accident and not considered in any way to be a contributory cause. Afterwards No A800 was reported as having been removed to Ashford on its own wheels. The engine remained in this state for some eight months before rebuilding as a 'U' class tender engine commenced on 2nd May 1928. The work was not completed until 15th December, the time taken being longer than it had been to convert any of the other members of the class.*

As is known, riding tests were carried with members of the class on both the SR and LNER main lines, reportedly with Nigel Gresley on the footplate. Recent research has revealed slightly more than appeared in the Board of Trade report concerning these trials, as not only was Gresley present but also it appears Bulleid, then of course still with the LNER. On one of the SR trials Gresley it appears, demanded the engine be slowed and refused to travel on it further. No such reluctance was displayed by Bulleid!

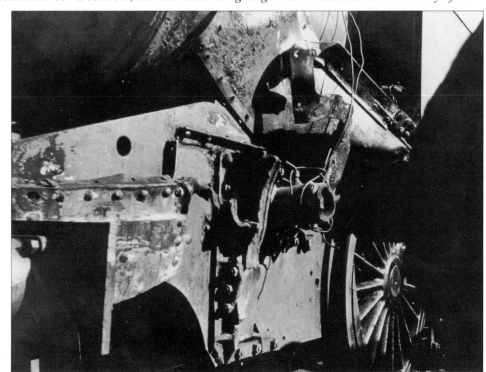

Eustace Missenden, left ,as London District Traffic Superintendent for the SECR sometime between 1920 and 1923; and below, in 1936, as Traffic Manager for the Southern Railway. In his favour was that he had risen from the bottom and was to inspire loyalty through reward. It worked, it was said, most of the time. Against him, was a cold attitude and apparent distrust of politicians and civil servants. During his tenure as General Manager at Waterloo he did not serve in the Home Guard although the SR Chairman, Rob Holland-Martin and Missenden's deputy, John Elliot, both did. Missenden tasked Elliot in the form. When the railways were requested to form Home Guard units, Missenden tasked Elliot in this form, "Now J B (Elliot) you were a Sandhurst man and know the Army's way of doing things, go up to the War Office....", hence Missenden was adept at choosing the right man for the job. For Missenden, this period was also spent shuttling between the wartime SR Headquarters at Deepdene, near Dorking, Waterloo and the REC London Headquarters. Upon taking charge at the nationalised Railway Executive, there are conflicting reports concerning his view of Bulleid's Tavern Car design. Some say he was in favour, although Sir John Elliot in his own auto biography 'On and Off the Rails' records that initially Missenden reacted only mildly although after riding in one he ordered they be sent back to Eastleigh to be fitted with proper windows. Despite also having maintained warm relations with Bulleid whilst on the Southern, these appeared to have cooled somewhat by1949. Perhaps this was because Missenden was no longer at Waterloo, or perhaps even he felt Bulleid was going off at a tangent. Whatever, it was noted that at the presentation to mark Bulleid's retirement, it was John Elliot who was in charge.

MAN OF THE SOUTHERN
SIR EUSTACE MISSENDEN
O.B.E. M.Inst.T.

Pick up any railway book relative to the history of the Southern Railway from 1939 onwards and two men feature prominently. One of course is Oliver Bulleid, the second Eustace Missenden. Interest in the first is understandable, an engineer of undoubted ability but one whose ideas may not have been truly appropriate to the time. (A new book 'Bulleid, the Man, the Myth, the Machines' has been completed and is due for publication in mid-2010). Missenden, though his name may be familiar, is not nearly so well known. As General Manager of the SR from 1939 until 1947, his was the task to steer the railway through its most difficult days, as well as defending his Chief Mechanical Engineer from contemporary criticism.

Eustace James Missenden reached the top job on the Southern aged 53, with effect from 25th September 1939. According to contemporary press reports, this was in the dual role of General Manager and Traffic Manager, although this might appear slightly strange. Certainly by 1940 the very capable R M T (Dickie) Richards was in the latter role and may well have been so earlier. So far as Missenden was concerned, it was the culmination of a career that had commenced on the SECR in 1899, at the tender age of 13. It was also a case of a 'early-school lever made good', but which, according to both John Elliot and Michael Bonavia, also gave him a 'chip on his shoulder', with a distrust of public school men.

Eustace Missenden had been born on 3rd March 1886, the son of James Missenden the station master at Bekesbourne, near Canterbury and it was here that the young Eustace's career began. We know he would sit in the station booking office with his father which was where he first started to learn the railway business. No doubt this early grooming by his father prior to his official starting time helped, for he was quick to learn all aspects of station working(s) and was transferred, aged 20, to the office of the Superintendent of the Line in March 1906. Again he must have excelled, for six years later in June 1912 he was appointed Assistant to the District Superintendent of the Eastern Division at Ashford. It was in the same year, 1912, that he married Lillian Adeline Gent. Two years later came another promotion as Assistant to the London District Superintendent.

Further promotion followed, in May 1919 as Acting London District Superintendent, a role he took on fully succeeding H E O Wheeler in July 1920. Shortly after the grouping he became Divisional Operating Superintendent London (East) and then Assistant Superintendent of Operations in 1930. (Missenden was just one of several former SECR men to be given senior positions on the newly created Southern Railway).

It was at this stage in his career that it became apparent he was being singled out for one of the highest roles, as, no doubt to gain the widest experience, he became Docks and Marine Manager in 1933 and then in 1936, consequent upon the merger of the commercial and operating departments, he took over from E C Cox as Traffic Manager. (We can only imagine this must have been a difficult role for Missenden, as he found difficulty in dealing with the French over the cross-Channel services.)

From 1923 onwards, all of these moves had been made at the instigation of Sir Herbert Walker, who, as General Manager certainly would not take on a dual role in charge of traffic as well. It is for this reason that it is felt likely that the Traffic Manager role was removed from Missenden shortly after he took the chair at Waterloo in 1939. It would appear that when offered the role by the Southern Railway Chairman, Rob Holland-Martin, the post had indeed been designated that of Acting General Manager, on the premise that Szlumper might well return. Missenden evidently refused to accept this, threatening instead to remain as Traffic Manager or resign unless he was offered the substantive post. It was thus that he became General Manager.

Missenden's strengths were those of being a competent railwayman, a good organiser who knew how to delegate and who looked after the interests of subordinates who served him well. Well versed in operating, if he had a weakness it was relative to the commercial side of management. Perhaps this may explain why he was so keen to support Bulleid, who was thus able to convince Missenden over the operational merits and needs of a proposed design. He was used also to the various department heads reporting to him, something that did not occur when he was later the first Chairman of the newly formed Railway Executive.

To his senior staff he lacked both the character and charisma of his immediate predecessor Gilbert Szlumper and certainly that of Sir Herbert Walker, although he was known to admire the latter greatly. For a man in such a senior position it is slightly strange to relate that he was suspicious of both politicians and civil servants. Michael Bonavia puts this down to his lack of formal education. It no doubt also contributed to his limited ability at expressing himself well on paper - except so far as railway jargon was concerned. Personality-wise he was cold and whilst tough morally he was adverse to working long hours and reportedly fastidious over his own health.

The rationale behind Missenden's appointment in 1939 was that Gilbert Szlumper had been transferred to be Director General for Transportation and Movements at the War Office and Missenden not only replaced him at Waterloo, but also took on the role as a member of the Railway Executive Committee. He remained in charge at Waterloo until October 1947, handing over the reigns to John (later Sir John) Elliot, whose own tenure was of course destined to be brief, before the General Manager role was superseded by the new title of Chief Regional Officer. (The title 'General Manager', but of course now applicable to a Southern Region not a Southern Railway, would be reinstated later).

Elliot, had previously held the post as principal Assistant to Szlumper but upon Missenden's appointment become the Deputy General Manager. This may have been considered a necessity due to the amount of war work being undertaken by Missenden, whilst also allowing for an immediate successor in the event of accident. Together Missenden and Elliot made a formidable team, Missenden a careful, competent and experienced railwayman but certainly not a warm personality. In Elliot there was a man totally the opposite in character to Missenden and who was seen as a man of the world with

numerous outside contacts. They forced a strong alliance, with none of the power struggle that might otherwise have been expected under the circumstances..

On the Southern itself and despite having been a protagonist in favour of electrification in Sussex and Kent, Missenden's relations were warmer towards Bulleid than towards the electrical engineer Arthur Raworth. This may perhaps go some small way to explaining why Bulleid was able to forge ahead with his own ideas, although it must be acknowledged that authorisation for a steam design was easier and of course cheaper than for a complete electrification scheme. Part of Missenden's enthusiasm towards Bulleid may have come from the latter's charm, although make no mistake, when harsh decisions needed to be made, such as when the unreliability of the new 'Merchant Navy' class meant there was the risk of traffic disruption in the London area, Missenden was quick to issue an edict banning the class from working east of Salisbury until matters were resolved. Although accepting it without question we know Bulleid did not respond to this well.

Although having accepted the chairmanship of the Railway Executive following nationalisation, Missenden's private intention had always been to retire before too long which he did with effect from the end of December 1950. He was awarded an O.B.E in 1937 and a Knighthood (Knight Bachelor) in the Birthday Honours of 1944. Further honours followed, KStJ; Officer of Legion

Opposite page - On 15th February 1949 at Waterloo Battle of Britain 4-6-2 No 34090 was named 'Sir Eustace Missenden'. Those present read almost like a 'whos - who' from the contemporary Southern scene, left to right, T E Chrimes, Motive Power Superintendent; H L Smedley, Legal Advisor and Solicitor Railway Executive; W J England, ex-Superintendent of Operation; H E O Wheeler, ex-Superintendent of Operation; R G Davidson, ex-Chief Accountant; O W Cromwell, Chief Officer for Labour and Establishment; R M T Richards OBE, Deputy CRO; Sir Eustace Missenden, O V S Bullied, CME; John Elliot, Chief Regional Officer; S W Smart OBE, Superintendent of Operations; R P Biddle CBE, Docks and Marine Manager; C Graseman, Public Relations and Advertising Officer.
This page - top, The guard of honour at the naming ceremony, made up of SR men and women of all grades and who gave 'good service' in WW2. *Right* - Presentation at Waterloo. The man with the braided cap was Mr Savage, Guildford Station Master, in the trilby, Lengthman G H Leach of Aldershot. Both Messrs Savage and Leach had been awarded the George Medal for service in wartime.

of Honour (France); Chevalier, Order of Leopold (Belgium); American Medal of Freedom with Gold Palm. Also in 1949, he was made Colonel-Commandant of the Engineer and Railway staff Corps, R.E. (T.A), although details of what was an obvious association with the military are limited. The only information that has come to hand relative to this, is in his organisation of transport for the outward journey of the B.E.F. and the subsequent return from Dunkirk. This must have come especially hard to him, for he possessed a narrow outlook on life with a dislike of foreigners, none more so than the French and he had no sympathy for them in 1940. He was a founder member and former vice-president of the Institute of Transport. In addition to his railway connections, he was, in November 1946, reported as being a director of the following businesses; Thomas Cook and Son Ltd., Hay's Wharf Cartage Co. Ltd., Pickfords Ltd., Carter Paterson and Co. Ltd., Chaplins Ltd., Norman E. Box Ltd., Garlick Burrel and Edwards Ltd., and the East Kent Light Railways Company.

His resignation letter to both Sir Cyril Hurcombe of the British Transport Commission and to Alfred Barnes, Minister of Transport, appeared in *The Times* for 23rd December 1950 together with replies from each. All were polite, yet expressed in formal terms, acknowledging his work undertaken both on the Southern, during war time and for three years under the nationalised organisation.

At this stage Missenden was aged 64, and would be able to enjoy 22 years in retirement. He died aged 86, on 30th January 1973 having been a widower for 14 years.

Opposite page - Waterloo, February 1949. **This page, top left** - In charge at Waterloo on 21st August 1947, a press photograph depicting 'Britain's New Railway Chief', the day after his appointment as Chairman of the nationalised Railway Executive was announced by Mr Alfred Barnes, Minister of Transport. **This page top right** - 34090 in working condition, depicted at Stewarts Lane, on 25th September 1949. At this time it was allocated to Ramsgate but was transferred to the Stewarts Lane fleet in May 1951. Rebuilt between June and August 1960, it survived in traffic until the very end of steam in July 1967 and was cut up at Cashmore's, Newport in March 1968. **Below** - 14th December 1966, Sir Eustace, (right) making his acceptance speech after being presented with one of the nameplates from 34090 by the then General Manager of the Southern Region, David McKenna OBE. At this stage the engine was still in service. His pastimes were listed as golf and gardening. *Photographs; RCHS Spence Collection - 4, and KR Archive - 5.*

A BRIGHTON SUBURBAN TRAIN OF THE 1870s.

This posed view depicts Stroudley Terrier No. 75 'Blackwall' with a set train of eight close-coupled suburban coaches. It was probably taken early in 1873 when they were brand new – they are clearly ex-works with white roofs and tyres. The train has been brought here to have its photograph taken as a record of the new suburban stock then entering service.

The location is on the east coast line near Brighton, to the east of Ditchling Road Tunnel, with the road bridge over Hollingdean Road visible on the right. The site is hard to recognise today as the hills behind the train were extensively built over in the later nineteenth and twentieth centuries. In the foreground is the single line of the Kemp Town branch which still looks newly laid, as indeed it was, the branch having opened in 1869. In later years, sidings would cover part of the area following the opening of Lewes Road station in September 1873.

The train comprises, from the left, a Brake Third, a Third, a Second, two Firsts, two Thirds and a Brake Third. The carriages represent the earliest design of Stroudley passenger stock with no compartment divisions and single lights in the Thirds. Later versions of the Seconds had four compartments rather than the five seen here. Interestingly, the brake carriages have Mansell wheels like those of the other carriages; in later years, most brakes had spoked wheels. The extremely large headboards for the South London line whose lettering states London Bridge, Denmark Hill, Clapham,

NOTES BY JOHN MINNIS

Wandsworth, York Road (renamed Battersea Park in 1885) and Victoria are decidedly non-standard and one wonders whether they were simply applied for the purpose of this official photograph and never actually used in traffic. Certainly, the well-known view of No. 40 '*Brighton*' on a South London line train, which is of similar date, shows a much smaller headboard that extends only over the double doors for the guard. The photograph illustrates precisely the type of train the Terriers were intended to work on the South London and East London lines.

No. 75, which entered traffic in December 1872 and is seen here as built without the familiar Westinghouse pump on its cabside (the early members of the class gained this in 1879-82, according to D. L. Bradley), was sold to the Isle of Wight Central Railway in March 1899 and was withdrawn as Southern Railway No. W9 in 1926. The early Stroudley suburban carriages, which were described by J. Pearson Pattinson in 1898 as being 'very scantily furnished', were mostly withdrawn around 1900 – a body of a Brake Third of this type survives in good condition at Slindon.

Top - *Up starting signals as brought into use at Yeovil Junction on 2nd December 1951.*
Irvine Cresswell
A youthful Peter Squibb, complete with test equipment, recorded on Holes Bay curve, circa 1959.

'SOUTHERN EXPOSURE'

Peter Squibb

The year 1950 brought a much resented break in the continuity of railway service for my family. My great-grandfather, Frank Puckett, was an Engineering Department ganger with the Great Western Railway and almost certainly had some involvement with the final removal of the broad gauge in the West Country in 1892. His son-in-law, George Squibb, was a mason in the Building Department at Weymouth until his call-up and death during the Great War and my father, the sixth of his seven children, worked his way up through the grades of the GWR Operating Department until, in 1946, he was appointed to the signal box at Maiden Newton in Dorset. Had he stayed at Dauntsey, between Wootton Bassett and Chippenham, many things would have been very different and our publisher would never have requested these reminiscences of my experience with the Southern Region.

The nationalisation of the railways in 1948 was not so traumatic for the staff as the so-called rationalisation which followed two years later. A bureaucratic decision saw boundaries drawn on the map of the United Kingdom, one that divided the country's railways arbitrarily into geographic areas and which took little or no account of operating requirements. Suddenly, all lines south of the Western Region main line from Reading to Exeter were transferred to the Southern Region and some severe culture shocks were registered. The Midland & South Western Junction was one line so affected and became Southern from Savernake to Andover, until yet another high level decision caused it to be returned to the W.R.

Difficult operating procedures became manifest. Some would have been amusing had they not been so fatuous, but the men on the ground shrugged their shoulders and got on with the job of running a safe railway. When I began my employment in October 1954, I was thoroughly "Southern" but readers may be able to detect a certain in-bred prejudice!

Mr Compton, the Signal & Telecommunications Department Inspector at Exeter Central travelled to Maiden Newton with a form for me to fill in. It was the first of many! Then I was sent to Southampton Terminus so that the Railway Medical Officer could check that I had all my bits and pieces and that they were all in the right places.

Initially I was to work with the Telegraph Lineman based at Yeovil Pen Mill, whose district stretched from Maiden Newton including the Bridport Branch, to Sparkford with the Yeovil to Taunton Branch as far as Thorney and Kingsbury Halt. Bernard Lock was not long out of the R.A.F. when I started but he was a natural railwayman and an excellent teacher. More significantly, he had built a portable model railway for his son and had constructed his own pointwork, which impressed me mightily. He showed me how to solder, it was part of the job, but had considerable implications for my life-long passion for scale modelling.

The railway history of the Yeovil area is quite complex but it resulted in three "Yeovil" stations. Yeovil Junction is on the Southern main line from Waterloo to Exeter and is located a couple of miles south of the town. Yeovil Pen Mill is the former Great Western station on the Weymouth line. It was also a junction as a branch of the Bristol & Exeter Railway linked Taunton with Pen Mill running through Langport, Martock and Yeovil Town. There was a siding at Pen Mill called the "B&E", but I don't suppose too many of the staff there had any idea what the initials stood for 75 years after the company was absorbed by the Great Western.

As its name suggests, Yeovil Town was close to the shopping centre and, almost inevitably, no longer exists. Besides the Great Western trains to Taunton, it also saw a frequent shuttle service to Yeovil Junction. It was a not a joint station with staff on site from both companies, as all employees there were Southern men but the signalling, including the signal box, had been supplied by the G.W.R. and was maintained by the linemen at Pen Mill.

It was in Yeovil Town signal box that I saw my first Preece's block instrument, an ancient affair, massively built with very little internal mechanism, just a simple solenoid which operated a miniature lower quadrant signal arm and gave but two indications. "Line Clear" was understood by the arm being down, for "Train on Line" and "Line blocked" or "Normal", the arm was

SR / Bulleid diesel-electric 10202 at Weymouth, circa 1952.   *Ron Hersey collection.*

horizontal. I was to learn that this was a "three wire" system, meaning that between signal boxes there was a wire for the "Up Block" (indications for trains in one direction), one for the "Down Block" and one for the block bell. The three circuits shared a common return, originally "earth" but a metallic return came to be preferred. Little did I know at that time that this was just one of several block systems in use on the Southern Railway; I was to encounter a few of them over the years.

By this time my father had obtained a Relief Signalman's position and consequently could be found working any of the 'boxes on our district (except one) and indeed very much further afield. Despite the regional boundary that now existed between Castle Cary and Sparkford, the area overseen by the District Inspector at Yeovil Pen Mill was as it had always been, so dad worked as far as the Frome area, including Mells Road and Radstock on the North Somerset line. By now his uniform cap bore a green badge. His fellow relief-man, Jimmy Bant, was based at Castle Cary and would arrive for work at Pen Mill 'box sporting a brown cap badge!

Where the line to Weymouth and the Yeovil Town to Junction branch ran side by side, a new signal box had been built during World War 2 to work crossovers between the two companies' lines, so that Paddington to Exeter trains could be diverted in emergencies. The 'box saw little use but my father added it to his list and when working it would be in contact with Pen Mill, Yetminster, Yeovil Town and Yeovil Junction "A". This meant that he was "passed out" for Yeovil Pen Mill, Yeovil South Junction and Hendford Goods but not Yeovil Town which sat between the three. That was a Southern 'box: but weren't we all Southern? The silliness existed for more years than it should have done.

About the beginning of 1957 a new signal box was built which superseded Weymouth Station and Junction 'boxes. This was the last large mechanical box commissioned by the Southern Region, and had over 100 levers. My mate, Bernard Lock, was given the task of wiring the lever frame and its associated relays. He was to be assisted by Derek Hopkins, my opposite number at Yeovil Junction. This meant some juggling of staff in the Yeovil area and involved some temporary (but long term) upgrading. I was to be acting Assistant Lineman (Dual) Class 2. The Assistant Signal Lineman at Pen Mill was also upgraded to Class 2 from Class 3. My basic weekly wage rose from £3:5 shillings to £13:12 shillings, his went from £13:10 to £13:12! As we left the meeting where all

78

this was explained and headed for the café, he made it clear that I was buying the teas. He bore no grudge as far as I was concerned as none of the arrangements were of my doing but he was not happy.

The weekend that saw the new 'box commissioned at Weymouth was something of a disaster. My father and I travelled from Maiden Newton on the last passenger train. He was to act as one of many "Groundmen" while the signals were transferred from the old 'boxes to the new one. (By now we should have referred to them as "Handsignalmen" but we were slow to learn to speak "Southern"). I was detailed to connect several sets of electric point detectors, but because of everything else that was going on, it was difficult to get the points operated from the lever frame for testing and the whole job, not just my bit, took much longer than expected.

The Inspector in charge had advised me to have my bike with me, as the operation would be complete long before the first train on the Sunday morning. In the event my dad did eight hours "flagging", went home for eight hours rest and came back again to find me still working but struggling to stay awake. I was eventually released to catch the 5.35 pm train, having been on duty since midnight. The new 'box was eventually up and running sometime on the Monday morning, but to their credit every wire that Bernard and Derek had installed was correct. Most of the problems that I recall, was with new track circuits that were short-circuited as track settled to sit on new point rodding.

With the Weymouth job completed, Bernard was able to resume his duties at Yeovil Pen Mill and I was then used to cover holidays and sickness at Weymouth and Yeovil Junction, so for a lot of the time was receiving "higher grade pay". It was a severe blow when I was not needed to do this and had to revert to my "Learners" wages.

Relieving at Yeovil Junction had its compensations, and not just the extra money. It meant that Yetminster was a short cycle ride away and one of my better moves had been to attract the attention of a lovely secretarial student who travelled from there to college in Yeovil by train. She has proved to be very much more than an expert typist.

The telegraph lineman at the Junction was on extended sick leave so his assistant was upgraded and I spent some months making up the numbers. It was like starting my service again in some respects as a lot of the equipment was different to the Western instruments that Bernard had explained to me.

The up-graded assistant was more keen on horse racing than signal and telegraph apparatus and often left me to get on with the maintenance while he sorted out his "winners". His district included the Chard branch, which was transferred to the Southern Region in 1950 and I recall I volunteered to check the Thornfalcon token batteries at Creech Junction one day. Access was via

Yeovil Town and Martock, then a short walk from Creech St. Michael Halt. The battery maintenance took but a few minutes and I had an hour or two with the signalman watching 'Kings', 'Castles', 'Granges' and other Swindon products on the four-track main line. What a way to get paid - but I must remember that this is a publication for Southern enthusiasts.

One thing the bookies' friend did explain to me was the working of the Preece's "one wire block instrument" This was housed in a similar case to the one I saw at Yeovil Town, but as the name implies, utilised just one wire with earth return, to accommodate the block indications for both directions as well as the bell codes.

If my memory is reliable after fifty years, the crucial piece of the mechanism was a swinging armature that received a magnetic characteristic from an electromagnet suspended just above it. The polarity of the electromagnet was decided by the Block Switch at the other end of the section. Unfortunately, the armature developed a slight permanent magnetism over the years and would stick to one of the pole pieces of the bell coils instead of swinging between the two. The usual cure was to wrap a piece of cored solder around the favoured pole piece and gradually all our instruments were being so treated. This idiosyncrasy gave me an experience that is fresh in my mind even though half a century has fled.

The stations west of Yeovil Junction were Sutton Bingham and Crewkerne, but between the two sat Hardington Signal Box which existed purely to shorten the section. Just after lunch one day, we received a call from Hardington to say that the instrument working with Sutton Bingham was displaying the symptoms just described. This constituted a block failure and all up trains were being stopped and told to pass the up starting signal at danger. Hardington was a 'day turn only' box, but the signalman could not close it while a failure existed, so his request for attention was especially urgent. He could envisage being there all night if we could not help.

My mate became very agitated. He was going out somewhere after work and was worried that we would be late back. So off I went. Very conveniently a down goods train was about to leave, so arrangements were made for me to be set down at Hardington. I guess the signalman was always pleased to have company as his box was very remotely situated, but I was made particularly welcome. On a couple of occasions I had been mistaken for a trespassing schoolboy in the Yeovil area, but this fellow greeted me with enthusiasm.

The problem was the old perennial one, so I carried out the usual remedy and after thorough testing began to wonder how I was going to get home. The signalman had his bike but I was stuck; there was no chance of another convenient goods train or light engine. The next up train was the 4.30 Exeter, first stop Yeovil Junction and treated by the staff with the sort of reverence that the Western men reserved for the 'Limited'.

However, Southern regulations were going to

Yeovil Town - Pen Mill straight ahead and Yeovil junction to the right. (Peter was at pains to point out the railwayman on the right is not him!)   *The Lens of Sutton Association*

come to my rescue! When a block failure had been rectified, it was deemed necessary to send a "Clearance Ticket" to the signal box in advance, a practice only observed by the G.W.R. after a complete break-down of communications. This was not the time to discuss the rationality of stopping one more train than was necessary as it was going to work in my favour. The signalman was seriously concerned about stopping the 4.30, but I pointed out that without the clearance ticket the failure still existed so he could not clear his starting signal.

He bit the bullet and soon received the bell signals as the "fast" passed Crewkerne dead on time and I made my way to the up Home signal with the ticket. Very soon the deep bellow of a Bulleid Pacific could be heard as the Distant signal was approached and then the train appeared, still blowing, and I could see the driver and fireman (and lots of passengers) peering in my direction. As the engine stopped I nipped up the ladder - Bulleid Pacifics had ladders not steps, and on to the footplate. The signal came off as I did so and I quickly explained the situation to the driver.

The gradient was quite severely against the train but for the next few minutes I was treated to an exhibition of footplate skills that I have never forgotten. The driver began to coax his machine into motion, as he inched the regulator open he was leaning out listening for the first sound of slip from the 'Merchant Navy's' driving wheels. When it happened he closed the regulator, applied some

sand and opened it again. Very soon he had the heavy train rolling and he looked at me.

"In a lot of years on this run, that's the first time I've seen those signals anything but "off". The fireman joined in, "We were doing a ton too". I grinned, "Not hanging about then". The driver saw my scepticism. "He's not kidding." he said. By now I was sitting on the fireman's seat as he needed space to swing his shovel. That too was worth watching as with superb precision he fed his hungry fire.

I threw out the clearance ticket as we blasted through Sutton Bingham and we soon rolled to a stop at Yeovil Junction. The incident had meant that the train was at least ten minutes late as I bade farewell to my new friends but they had accepted the situation with equanimity and we parted on the best of terms. As far as I know, I never saw them again.

It was a very impressive performance by two consummate professionals and their machine, a type of engine about which I had previously been habitually scathing.

Because I had spent a lot of my boyhood in signal boxes, I was very familiar with the way they were worked, (probably more so than I should have been) and I quickly cultivated those signalmen who were happy to let me have a go. Although it was forbidden, it was a big help as far as my job was concerned to know how the equipment was used. And I enjoyed it immensely! There was a strange

Sherborne, the location of the incident involving the Royal Blue coach described below.

Seen here is the new box, commissioned in 1961 and on the opposite side of the line to the original box in use during Peter's time. The co-acting arms for the Up Starting signal, No 6, were necessary due to visibility restrictions caused by the station footbridge.

'S15' No 30832 is arriving at the station with the Sunday 1.03 pm Salisbury to Exeter stopping service, 12th November 1961.

Harold Ball

anomaly related to this. Large busy signal boxes often employed "booking boys" whose duty it was to keep the "Train Register" up to date, recording the times of every movement and incident. Like me, they were forbidden to operate the levers and instruments, but by the time they moved into a signalman's position they were expected to be competent. Most inspectors turned a blind eye as they had probably travelled the same route, but there were some who would creep up on signal boxes from unexpected directions to catch the staff being naughty. If I was observed doing it, the procedure was to pretend that there had been some trouble with the equipment and I was testing it!

One senior relief signalman in the Yeovil Junction area was always glad to see me, so that he could read the newspaper and I could do his job. I was doing that at Sherborne one day when he suddenly said, "Quick, wind 'em up, here comes the opposition!"

The old signal box was opposite the site of the later one and gave a good view of the town. Reg had spotted the Royal Blue coach to London, making its way towards the level crossing and although the next down train had only just left Templecombe, I did as I was told. The coach came to a stand at the gates and the driver got out and leaned his elbows on the top rail. "I don't suppose it's left London yet!" he shouted.

"That's done it," said Reg, "He can stay there another ten minutes now!" He did too!

I was fully expecting to do National Service; lads in my year at school were disappearing from circulation as their call-up papers arrived, but I'm still waiting for mine. I registered, had the medical examination and a difference of opinion with an army officer who refused to believe that my employer would consider that I had resigned if I signed on to do three years in his army rather than the mandatory two. I had to go back to work and find out the facts and then write to him with British Railways' stance on the matter. The answer was as I had told him and he replied that it was very short-sighted of B.R. as, in his opinion, the extra year of drill, weapon training and foreign travel would make me a more efficient member of the S&T department.

Many years have passed and I have heard nothing from the War Department. B.R. never told me that they had negotiated a "reserved occupation" status for me, but as I was constantly relieving at both Yeovil depots and at Weymouth I can only conclude that that was what happened. Either that or my details were left on a train by a civil servant and never seen again. Did they do that sort of thing in the 1950s?

1948 and all that...

The 1948 locomotive exchanges witnessed unusual workings both on and off the region. So far as the Bulleid breed was concerned, two 'Merchant Navy' class locomotives, Nos 35017 and 35019, were set to work away from the SR, and No 35018 on the SR. 35020 was retained as a spare. It was not needed to travel further afield. Three of the 'West Country' type were also tested, Nos 34004. 34005 and 34006. All the engines involved were prepared at Eastleigh which included light repairs and of course the necessary fitments for subsequent dynamometer car tests. A necessity was the swap of the Bulleid tender for one of 'Stanier' design. This was dictated by the longer non-stop runs the engines would be expected to perform which in turn required the use of water pick-up gear. From an aesthetic perspective it was a shame that seven especially cleaned and prepared green engines were matched with black painted tenders. Elsewhere it has been mentioned that the provision of a strange tender could be a distinct disadvantage to the fireman, but this does not seem to have affected the men involved.

Opposite top - 34006, 'Bude' with its trademark long smoke deflectors, at Marylebone awaiting departure for Manchester in what was considered to be the 'General Purpose Engine' group, better known as 'Mixed Traffic'. In this area 34006 was pitted against a 'Black 5' and a 'Hall' although elsewhere, but not from Marylebone, a 'B1' was also involved in the same group. The same engine would also be tested between Taunton and Plymouth.

Opposite bottom - 35019 *'French Line CGT'* being prepared at Eastleigh in April 1948. At this time the engine was supposedly just over three years old, having officially entered traffic on 7th June 1945 although a recently found photograph purports to depict the engine brand new and complete at Eastleigh on 20th February and captioned on the reverse as due to receive the name, *'Compagnie Generale Transatlantique'*. All the Pacifics selected for test had recently been outshopped but were taken back in for checking and preparation which included a wedge-fronted cab if one had not already been fitted.

Above - Receiving less in the way of attention were the freight test carried out between Bristol and Eastleigh via Salisbury in August and September 1948. Five engines types were involved, 'Austerity' 2-10-0 and 2-8-0 type, and WR, LMS and ER 2-8-0s. Here 'O1' 2-8-0 No 63789 waits at Eastleigh before taking on what was considered to be the relatively easy westbound run. In the opposite direction none of the engines tested managed to keep to the schedule, although the best runs were recorded with the 'Austerity' type.
With grateful thanks to Chris Mileham (1) and Rod Blencowe (2).

The testing of passenger workings on the Southern involved the Waterloo - Exeter route, although it was really only once beyond Salisbury that there was ever any real need to work the engines hard. Four types were involved, the home grown 'Merchant Navy', an 'A4', LMS 'Duchess' and an LMS 'Royal Scot'. It is the latter that is seen here, in the shape of 46154 'The Hussar', **top left** at Waterloo after arrival from Exeter and **bottom left**, in the reverse direction passing Andover at speed with the line from Stockbridge trailing to the right. This locomotive was in the hands of Driver Brooker of Camden - as ever the poor fireman's name is omitted, although both contributed to some credible performances from what was the smallest of the engines tested. Again a non-standard tender has been fitted, the pairing being with an 8-wheel type from an 'Austerity'.

Right - Weighing the ashes and clinker from 38xx No 3803 at the end of the run. This type of exercise was undertaken on all the engines participating and added considerably to the work involved. In a desire to reduce coal consumption to a minimum, some crews made the decision not to exert their engines and which led to a number of inferior trips compared with what might otherwise have been expected. The view was taken by the late S C Townroe at Eastleigh.

Again with grateful thanks to Chris Mileham (1) and Rod Blencowe (2).

Below - Received just in time for inclusion was this view of 35020 'Bibby Line' complete with LMS tender No 10373 but at the unmistakable location of Southampton Central.
Paul Watkins collection.

STOCK STORAGE ON THE ARDINGLY BRANCH

Of all the articles and illustrations that have appeared in 'Southern Way' since we started, none has created greater interest than that concerning the storage of rolling stock on the Ardingly Branch as appeared on page 88 of 'Issue 5'. In consequence we have persuaded Roger Merry-Price to provide further details from his archive and it is with pleasure that these are reproduced over the next few pages together with a selection of appropriate photographs from the Bluebell Archive - J J Smith collection. (Thanks to Tony Hillman).

BRITISH RAILWAYS - SOUTHERN REGION
District Traffic Superintendent's Office
London (Central) District
Redhill, Surrey.   Ref: R.113/3 R/N   12th September 1958.

Kent Coast Electrification: Stage 1, Phase 1 - Proposed berthing of empty electric stock on the Down line between Horstead Keynes and Ardingly.

"Further to my letter of the 8th instant under reference 'ST/BN' and your 'S1/Pad. Electric', I have given careful consideration to the signalling and permanent way alterations which will be required and hereunder my recommendations:-

Horstead Keynes.

1   The existing Down Line to be broken between the facing end of No 16 (Down line and Dock) Points and the trailing end of No 30 (Up Main to Ardingly) Points..
2   No 13 To Ardingly Advanced Starting signal arm to be removed.
3   Last Vehicle Treadle 'C' to be disconnected.
4   No 27 Up Main to Ardingly Starting signal to be released by No 30 (Up Main to Ardingly) points 'normal' and through the Electric Staff instrument, and to apply only to trains proceeding over the existing Up line.
5   No 38 From Ardingly Home signal to lock No 4 (up Main) points 'normal' instead of locking No 26 (FPL on 4) as at present.
6   No 40 From Ardingly Distant signal to be fixed, temporarily.
7   The conductor rail adjacent to No 33 Up Main Starting signal to be adequately ramped.
8   The Staffs in the Electric Train Staff Instrument, and at present inscribed 'Horstead Keynes and Culver Junction' to be altered to read 'Horstead Keynes and Ardingly'.

Ardingly

9   No 19 Down Distant signal to be suitably repositioned on the Up side of the line. This repositioned signal may remain fixed.
10   No 18 Down Home signal to be suitably repositioned on the Up side of the line to apply only when No 11 (Crossover points East) are reversed.
11   No 11 From Up Line Group signal to be removed.
12   Facing point lock and bar to be provided to lock No 11 (Crossover points East) when reversed and to apply for movements from the Up to the Down line.
13   No 5 Up Shunt Ahead signal to be disconnected.
14   No 3 Up Starting signal to be released through the Electric Train Staff Instrument.
15   Trap points to be provided on the Down Line, 290 yards on the Horsted Keynes side of Ardingly Signal Box.
16   The Electric Train Staff Instrument at present in Culver Junction Signal Box to be installed in Ardingly Box and the Staffs at present inscribed 'Culver Junction and Horstead Keynes' to be altered to read 'Ardingly and Horstead Keynes'

I shall be grateful if you will kindly pursue this matter with the Signal Engineer. I have requested the District Engineer, Brighton, to provide me with estimates for the work involved in items, Nos 1, 7, and 15.

W C Collins. District Traffic Superintendent.

Above - *Stock storage on the Ardingly line, 24th May 1959. New CEP set No 7137 leads a rake of similar units intended for Phase I of the Kent Coast electrification. (See article by Jeffrey Grayer in 'SW5'.) **Below** - By 30th August displaced steam stock was occupying the same spot. Set 951 was from the Hastings line, consisting seven vehicles, a brake composite at each end, then two thirds and a first class in the centre. The number of vehicles in the line up varied, although in 1962 no less than 144 were reported. Interestingly, whilst these were all subsequently condemned, there is reference to patrols to curb vandalism being undertaken. Was this also undertaken to protect the electric stock? (All Bluebell Archive / J J Smith)*

Southern Carriage and Wagon Society
Data Sheets - Section SL13
List of vehicles taken to Horstead Keynes following Kent Coast electrification 1959.

1.   To north of Horstead Keynes station: - set No 917, ie, 3553, 6642, 7963, 7966, 7974, 7976, 7979, 7980.
2.   Siding in station: - 3473, 4043, 1080, 6585, 4059, 5149, 4061, 194, 5595.
3.   Parked on line from Horstead Keynes to Ardingly, in order as follows (all condemned except those marked 'N', which were subsequently returned to traffic.
    (columns to be read downwards, not across: -

1101	3567	3673	5507	6565	5133	5509
968	5516	1023	3562	818 N	2332	980
4720	5528	1022	3587	819 N	2328	3569
1090	5515	1020	5527	7984	2325	6578 N
3545	985	3675	5526	7982	757	7967
5502	1153 N	1018	5524	7987	2341	4395
1141	843	1017	989	7981	4044	4397
1149	5529	3677	658	7909	7975	5155 N
3758	3570	1019	1131	5151	7210	4391
5668	1005	5595	3588	6566	7756	978
2754	5540	5578	786 N	3551	2326	4396
3549	4046	5579	7752	4394 N	2327	3589
3578	2348	3676	3548	7968	2340	3674
990	5530	1012	734	7965	7993	1029
993	762	1013	2349	7797	7986	1030
5521	811 N	4066 N	2350	7792	7992	1027
5512	5525	7960	2351	5651	7991	7422
996	4047	7910	2353	7908	3568	7421
5517	5532	979	5538	7794	983	1031
984	5531	992	5534	3549	5511	7419
994	2626	5508	5533	6582 N	5510	7420
3572	4654	5506	3577	5134	987	3672
		5505		2334		

Vehicles were not in all cases parked in set formation. All listed are corridor stock except 3473, 1080, 194, 1101, 968, 4720, 1090, 3545 (set 636) and 2626, 4654 (formerly Templecombe spares but out of use for about two years). Vehicles went direct to the HK line and from it to Newhaven, there being no connection with arrivals and departures at Gatwick or Hassocks.

Nondescript saloon S7797S photographed on Sunday 30th August 1959. All of these vehicles later ran as open seconds, witness the sealed doorways. Along with its neighbour, S7965S of similar type, both bear the condemned logo. Officially S7797S was withdrawn in July 1961, although according to David Gould in 'Maunsell's SR Steam Carriage Stock', No S7965S lasted until December 1961.

A page of similar vehicles. **Top right,** *S7992S on the same date but retaining early BR livery.*

Centre right *- S4396S. This was one of seven similar vehicles reclassified as 2nd in 1938 / 1939 and previously used in boat trains to the Kent coast. This particular vehicle had also been renumbered from 7906 at the time of reclassification.*

Bottom *- S7965S and S7797S, see caption lower left. The incredible line of vehicles is seen here to advantage, did such a sight exist ever exist anywhere else? Bearing in mind the comments made later, it is interesting to note that there is not a single obvious case of vandalism not for that matter, graffiti. The signal is the down distant for Ardingly, repositioned on the up side of the line and fixed at caution.*

What is not certain from the official notices and information concerning the storage of these vehicles is whether the current was switched off to the third rail on the former down line.

The list below is in standing order from Ardingly to Horstead Keynes; a line indicates a gap. Set numbers are shown where branded. Set numbers in brackets are not visibly branded.

Coach	Set	Coach	Set	Coach	Set
3668	341	5155	596 b (later in 468)	3752	222
3734	962	2793	760	3753	222
2765	444	1082		1168	
775	444	6237	714	3670	428
770	444	3467	714	2759	228
822	444	1144		5671	228
1132	434	1173		2760	228
1922	a	815		7213	436 d
3223	394	1057		1070	
5143	394	1061		971	
3222	394	1156		4050	470
———		813		3686	214 e
2771	234	5678		———	
812	234	759	432	3722	209
818	234 b	3736	199	1140	209
7211	431	2796	236	837	209
806	431	5683	236	1127	209
5665	(222)	5682	236	3723	209
2360	466	1170	236	7841	
835	466	1172	236	2758	227
2361	466	794	236	5670	227
836	466	2797	236	2757	227
2355		———		817	(444)
7400		3742	195	Tunnel	
1136		5644	195	1147	
765		3743	195	4394	b
1180	234	769	434 c	7789	431
4048	234	2359	218	798	431
1064		777	(432)	1135	431
1097		869		1130	
3554	468	814		783	432
1142	(468)	3664	440	3573	156
5591	(468)	803	426	2766	144
7409		4051		809	
840	207	5592		3671	428
1069	(156)	1139		785	432
1121		1167		5645	(962)
2769	233	3747	426	3735	962
1157	233	747	426	5640	268
1155	233	7962	426	833	(465)
1158	233	7209	426	658	b
1150	233	3746	426	1175	
2770	233	3666	459	5659	(247)
3716	204	5589	459	2798	803
5635	204	5587	459	2799	803
1134	204	3667	459	2354	
5656	204	3590	428	3740	194
820	204	1114			
5639	(241)	810	340		
———		3206	442		
1122	204				
3717	204				

Notes:
a - condemned at Eardley c2/1961
b - to Ardingly in 1959 purge, but not condemned - returned to traffic for further period.
c - withdrawn Eardley 1960.
d - originally condemned 2/1960.
e– see SN item 465.
Total number of vehicles above - 144.

Right - S7756S, a continental first brake vehicle, latterly running loose. Note especially the variations in width between the different vehicles. Bottom - S983S , an all third corridor with 64 seats and a lavatory at each end. Built at Eastleigh in early SR days for the South Eastern section these vehicles included a number of former SECR features including commode handles and door ventilators.
Both 30th August 1959.

Postscript - Further notes from the same Southern 'C & W' Society source reveal further movement of various items of stock.

March 1960 - 10 unidentified steam underframes at Horsted Keynes, ex Newhaven (all underframes previously stored at Horstead Keynes and Hassocks were eventually used; two steam frames were shortened at Lancing in 1957 though it is not known for what. On 13/4/1960 only 39 coaches remained at Horstead Keynes to be dealt with. Some of the Horstead Keynes coaches have returned to traffic, 3568, 3569 were in Stewarts Lane yard in March.

May 1960 - 6567 (ex set 29) and 6576 (ex set 23) and condemned coaches 7218, 7673, 7785, 7786 arrived from the south coast area on 3/5/1960. By 19/5/1960 6773, 7785, 7786 were at Newhaven being cut up. 320, an earlier arrival, and 6575 were taken to Horstead Keynes on 17/5/1960 and handed over to the Bluebell. By 19/5/1960 the Ardingly line comprised 994 - 3675. At the end near Horstead Keynes station were 23 underframes one of which wrecked an unidentified coach, awaiting scrapping, during a shunt move.

April 1961 - Underframes stored (mid March) south to north at Horstead Keynes, 2754, 1924, 7788, 7665, 6587, 1149, 1141, 5668 and 7399. At Horstead Keynes station, milk tank frame 4426, coach frames 1038, 1039, 6881, 6902, 6894, 6893 and 7220.

August 1961 - Just north of Ardingly station on 6/7/1961, 835, 836, 2360, 2361, 7392, 7397, 1388, 812 and it is believed 2771. Three other vehicles without numbers also noted.

December 1961 - Coaches at Eardley in November included 2354, 5640, 5659, 2798, 2799, 3740 and 3741. So far as is known, most of the coaches recently withdrawn via Eardley have passed to the Ardingly - Horstead Keynes line where 137 were counted on 19/11/1960. Probably due to vandalism , the line appears to be patrolled during daylight hours.

January 1962 - All the 144 coaches at Ardingly / Horsted Keynes have been condemned regardless of how recently shopped.

March 1963 - Ardingly - Horstead Keynes line on 29/7/1962, 23 coaches west of tunnel and 59 east of tunnel.

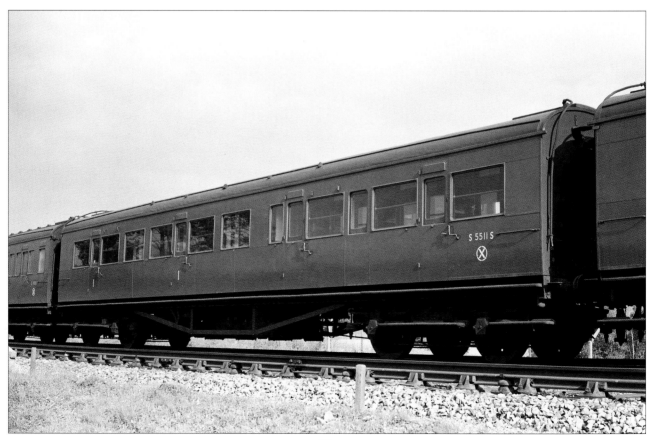

Right - *S2326S, a former LSWR 'Ironclad' from a 10-car set.* **Bottom** - *Eight compartment third No. S1030S of 1934. This was one of a batch originally numbered from 1019 to 1040 built to the restricted Hastings line loading gauge. No S1030S had formerly been in set No. 951.* **Opposite page** - *Corridor Composite S5511S, built at Eastleigh in May 1925 for use on the Eastern section. These vehicles had seven compartments with accommodation for 16 first and 24 third class passengers. A similar batch of vehicles was completed at Lancing around the same time. All - 30th August 1959.*

'REBUILDING' -THE LETTERS AND COMMENTS PAGE(S)

I do hope I can deflect a few of the brickbats received in recent months by the inclusion of a letters page this time. The reasons for there not being one, as had been genuinely intended in Issue 6, were referred to last time, the inclusion of extra pages in this issue reduces at least the pressure on available space. We will certainly try to make this a regular feature in the future.

Thank you all also for all your various comments, good, bad or indifferent. One thing that is immediately apparent is that the readership of 'SW' represents a wide cross-section of interest. Some like the early material, some prefer the late, some want more steam, some less. Bit like at home then, no matter what I do I get it wrong!

Seriously, the intention has always been to continue with the series provided three things continue, firstly it must a viable business proposition, secondly there must be a supply of worthwhile material and thirdly I must continue to enjoy it. Equally the support of our regular friends and helpers is required. I do not often get the chance to do this, but especial thanks then to Judi, Peter, Alastair, Bruce and Alan. No surnames are necessary, they know who they are. So far so good on all three counts.

Returning though to the comments received, (these are also welcome by letter, e-mail or telephone, although the latter may mean a scribbled note which cannot then be found when it is needed!), we received a welcome addition from Alan Morris of Milton Keynes back in January. (We should also thank Mrs Morris as well.)

- The early part of 2010 will see the release of a book on Southern Region Road Vehicles, more details shortly.

"In Issue 2 there is a photo of a Scammel somewhere in Watford. My wife was born in Watford, and on looking at the picture reckons it could have taken near the Hollywell Isolation Hospital. This was less than half a mile form the Scammel factory. My wife had memories of watching lorries leaving the factory with Scammels on their backs. Her Gran's house was quite close to the factory and the streets were narrow. As an aside, her mother worked in that very Hospital for a while. Now for a request, as a driver on the railway, I was briefly based at Charing Cross. I have an interest in the various EMUs used on the Southern. I know that steam will always be the first priority , I hope that future articles will cover electric units".

- EMUs have certainly not been deliberately omitted. We have a number of non-steam ideas 'bubbling', which will include more on the Southern Electric locos as well as the various Bulleid Diesel-Shunters. Note also Brian Golding's forthcoming book on SR EMUs referred to on the inside cover.

Roger Merry-Price, always a mine of information on rolling stock and workings generally has corrected his comment on page 89 of Issue 5. "The train in question is in fact the winter version of the 'Kentish Belle', comprising of ordinary BR or SR stock with the addition of a couple, or even three Pullmans in the formation."

As ever Eric Youldon has proved to be a veritable fount of knowledge. He has given me a veritable lashing re my comments in SW4 over Exeter Central, so here goes, "Exeter Central mystery photo? Don't think so! The Pacific on the three coach train has the Plymouth headcode and so is about to descend the incline to St Davids with an a M7 attached for a banking job a little later on. The Pacific at the rear has come down from Exmouth Junction to work westwards and has been 'tucked away' to clear the down main. When the Plymouth train has departed, the other Pacific will run down the platform to the carriage sidings (known as the field) to await its train. To suggest a failure is, I am afraid, typical

Nothing against copious views of 'Bulleid Pacifics' at all, but it is pleasing sometimes to secure a view of something different, especially when it is a unusual working. No prizes for guessing the unit of course, except to say it is not on the Brighton line. Instead a snapshot of the Royal Train passing through Liphook sometime in the 1950s. (We have access to a number of 'Grove' and 'Deepdene' records for the 1950s, but this does not appear to be one of them. Any further information would be welcome.)

Photo by Les Duffell, Booking Clerk at Liphook / Stephen Duffell collection.

'Cleaner boys' at Eastleigh, sometime around the period of the First World War. (The less than clean engine confirms the period.) We are always delighted to receive staff views for inclusion, this one a lovely example. All those shown had started as cleaners in 1908, forty years later they were drivers, still at Eastleigh. During WW1 some were also conscripted into a mounted home defence force. Left to right: Bob Radford, Bill Snook, George Roberts, Alec Ward (crouching), Sid Chalk and Charlie Godwin. Alec Ward was the father to Joyce, who later married Eastleigh man and 'Southern Way' contributor, Hugh Abbinnett. They are posed on the running plate of an 'H15'.

Joyce and Hugh Abbinnett

of the magazine's trend to denigrate the Bulleid Pacifics whenever an excuse arises. Steam drifting up from piping under the cab was uncommon with steam locomotives'.

- On the basis that I can only be hung once, I might add that I have prepared and submitted a manuscript, "Bulleid, the Man, the Myths, the Machines", due for release from Ian Allan / OPC in summer 2010. A few new revelations included and, not just for the benefit of Alan Morris, plenty on the 'Double Deck' units.

Eric Youldon, has also, amongst others, also pointed out that the MPD at Eastleigh could indeed be accessed from the down main line - see rear cover illustration on Issue 5.

Meanwhile I had only just finished, as I thought, these two pages, when Colin Chivers quite correctly pointed out the obvious, "I've only had a chance to flick through the pages so far but one photo stood out – the staff at Swanwick. As I'm sure others have already commented, I don't think either of your suppositions about the occasion are close – rather the photo was taken during one

of the pre-WW1 'strawberry seasons'. The guys in the straw hats are the giveaway – they are almost certainly the representatives of 'other railways' (LNWR, MR etc) sent to Swanwick for the 2-3 week season to supervise / assist with the paperwork and loading of the strawberry specials sent to their respective lines."

A slightly different opinion is expressed by Alastair Wilson of Chichester, "I would suggest that the date is 1905-1910 (so an association with the doubling in 1909 is entirely reasonable). The clues are as follows 1. The man immediately under the letter 'W', with his stand-up collar and tie, is wearing a slouch hat, which was the headgear worn by the City Imperial Volunteers in the Boer War. If you'd served out there, you wore your hat as a mark of distinction - so that puts the date as post-1902 2. Although the straw boater, as worn by the four 'gents' seated, came in (for boating) in the 1880s, by the first decade of the 20th century it was worn almost universally by middle-class men in summer. This again suggests 1900-1910 as a date. 3 The men's hairstyles: several have got a 'cowlick' (2nd from right, front row) or a 'quiff' (3rd from right, front row; under the letter 'N', and above the 'W', and above the 'K'). These styles were particularly popular 1905-14. 4   Front row seated, right hand end - his shapeless hat was particularly popular in the years 1910-14. All speculation, but I think a fairly educated guess."

To show also that I don't make it up, I am also berated by Dick Metcalfe Thomas, "I seriously think you should add a couple of pages to each issue, for <u>Readers Letters</u>, I accept that you do add edited items from your post-bag, but I feel there should be room for questions, reminiscences and answers from readers, you see lay men like me, who are non ex railwaymen. (Wouldn't accept me as I wear glasses!) There are articles that we would like more information on; or things that we'd like to know. I am old enough to remember and have travelled on the Southern Railway as a child, that is before the highway robbery of nationalisation, things like, in 1946 when my Father came home on leave, travelling from Portsmouth to Padstow for a holiday, and the last bit behind a T9! Plus going up to London in a 'Nelson', and things like that, if you were to think that there would be enough interest in reminiscences? I might be persuaded to try writing an article for you?" - *Yes please!*

Eric Youldon has also sent a number of valid comments on, well I could call them 'typo's, proofing errors, whatever. The BR Standard Tanks should be Class 3 not class 2, The H15 cannot be 336 and 21C25 should of course be 21C125. He also states that the view of 21C2 on page 81 is more likely to have suffered general wear and tear causing a loss of paint rather than a lagging fire. (Why do say lagging fires were unusual on a 'MN' Eric? Read on to find out.) Finally the other Eric, Eric Best has pointed out the date I could not find, the four coloured views of the 'Remembrance' class featured originally in the January 1936 issue of 'Railway Magazine'.

John Davenport, (his is the photograph seen as the double page spread on pages 2/3 of Issue 6), confirms my thoughts on the loco servicing area. "It was normally used by the Down Yard shunter, which was frequently 22 or 26. The latter in my youth was known as 'Old Squeaky Brakes' which was probably unkind. There is an M7 in the photo, but unusually facing east. If there was a station

No sooner had the ink hardly dried from issue 6, when Eric Youldon was in the post with this view of 34035 at Eastleigh in June 1963 and shortly after withdrawal. (See of course the colour cover view of 34035 on Issue 6). Eric quite correctly points out that 34035 only appeared with its modified front end for a short while, November 1959 to be precise and then further modified as per our cover illustration but with smoke deflectors added, in April 1960. It only remained in this form for a few months and was returned to traffic in conventional guise in October 1960.

Photo P H Groom

pilot or east side shunter, it faced that way. The Down yard Shunters always faced towards Guildford. More useless information". - *Don't you believe it, that is exactly the sort of thing we want! - Ed.*

As they say in the best regulated circles, "And now for something completely different". We have received the following which it is a pleasure to include in the hope someone may indeed be able to assist. Reader Arthur King from South Tottenham, is the owner of the left hand nameplate *'King Uther'*, which was attached to N15 No 737 from October 1925 until its withdrawal (as 30737) in June 1956. In common with such Southern plates, on the rear face it has the number of the locomotive to which it was allocated cast, (I think, but maybe stamped) into the brass. As can be seen in the photo, this plate displays the number 740 which has been scored through and then, to the left, the 'correct' number 737. Was *'King Uther'* originally to be allocated to 740, which in the event became *'Merlin'* in November 1925? Or was this no more than a cock-up in the casting department at Eastleigh? Maybe a Southern Way reader will be able to throw some light on this?' - *replies to the usual address please or via e-mail*

Now another request, does anyone have any information on the proposed but never built extension of the Chessington Branch through to Leatherhead? It has been suggested this is something we should cover in a future 'SW' but so far all enquiries have yielded little in the way of information. Again replies in the usual way, please.

Correspondence with Eric Youldon is always a pleasure and I have to report we have been exchanging

letters recently on the subject of lagging fires on the 'Merchant Navy' class. The subject having come up following my comment over a supposed fire on 21C2 as depicted on page 81 of Issue 6. Eric suggests this cannot be a lagging fire and that the 'MN' class were less prone to such episodes. Naturally I asked why and received the following answer, "I have to confess I cannot give a full answer except to say the early MNs had coupled wheel splashers which would have gone some way to arresting sparks flung up from brake blocks. It is a fact, even allowing for there being just 30 MNs against the 100 Light Pacifics, that the former were less prone to lagging fires than were their smaller brethren." Eric goes on to suggest poor paintwork is more likely as the metal casing still appears bright, a fire would cause a more rusty appearance. So there you have it, I sit corrected - unless of course YOU know different......?

A request from Mick Uden, a regular reader / contributor is more of the esoteric items that the Southern possessed; sludge tenders, is one of the examples he gives. Watch this space, we do have views of some such items. My excuse for now is this Issue is full up, but there is always No 8.

To finish with an unusual one. This sticker was found on the back of an 1890 handbill by Tony Hillman. (Others have also appeared from other sources.) 'Southern Railway Museum' - any ideas?

Terry Cole's Rolling Stock File No. 7
Some Electric Stock

Two of the three main constituents of the Southern railway had been pioneering the use of electric trains prior to the grouping in 1923. The London and South Western Railway had started to develop a system of electrified suburban lines using the ground level 3rd rail system whereas the London Brighton and South Coast Railway was using the technologically more advanced high voltage overhead system. When the Southern decided to standardise however it was cheaper to install the LSWR system which won out and the LBSCR system was dismantled.

As the Southern developed and extended its network of electrified lines it not only built a considerable quantity of new stock it also converted large quantities of older steam stock from all three companies primarily for suburban use.

Above - Here we see a returning Derby Day special at Tadworth on 30th May 1951 with 4-SUB unit 4174 leading. This unit is formed of ex-LSWR stock converted by the SR. The usual pattern for these steam stock conversions was to take whole trains of older coaches into the works, scrap the underframes (or in some cases reuse them for luggage vans), and remount the bodies on new longer underframes, adding compartments and new ends as necessary. By the early fifties these bodies were becoming life-expired so the units were progressively withdrawn, the bodies scrapped, and the underframes, which still had life in them, reused under newly constructed 'steel' EMUs. The 'Southern' wasted very little! The unit is showing the alphabetic code for a Tattenham Corner to London Bridge train. This system which originated on the LSWR was used on all the rebuilt sets until virtually the end of their existence. Bringing up the rear of the train is a Bulleid designed 4-SUB.

Opposite top - At the same location on the same day is another returning Derby Day special this time with Maunsell designed 4-LAV unit 2927 leading. 33 of these units were built primarily for the stopping and semi-fast services on the electrified 'Brighton' line. The term 4-LAV is a bit misleading as 3 of the 4 coaches were non corridor with no lavatories at all. Only one coach, the composite, was corridor and offered passengers access to this facility! This train is showing headcode 85, the numeric code for Tattenham Corner to London Bridge, the dual system existing side by side, finally being superseded when the last of the rebuilt units were withdrawn. Note also the ex-LBSCR lower quadrant signal on a concrete post. LBSCR lower quadrants were common even on the main lines at this period but were soon to be swept away.

Below - A view inside Lancing Carriage works with a Driving coach from 4 EPB unit 5026 undergoing overhaul. These sets, which marked a departure in the design of the ends from the previous Bulleid units, were built from 1951 onwards. They also had uprated electrical equipment enabling them to accelerate faster and electro-pneumatic self-lapping brakes. The standard Southern 'Buck-eye' couplers were fitted to the end of each unit. Inside however the passenger accommodation was very similar to the previous units.

[All photos Terry Cole collection]

John Hatherell was both a bridge and p/way engineer. Shortly after his move from Exeter, work took place on replacement of the old metal girders of Griffins Road Bridge. We do not know what if any involvement John had in the work, although as these views were located in his collection it was reasonable to assume he had some input. The date is shown as 30th September 1956.

THREE GENERATIONS OF RAILWAYMEN, IN THREE DIFFERENT DEPARTMENTS

LOCOMOTIVE, TRAFFIC and CIVIL ENGINEERING

JOHN HATHERELL

Three generations of my family have worked for the railways covering over a century from Victorian times through to the mid 1980s.

The first, my Grandfather Jesse, started as an Engine Cleaner at Swindon in 1877. He progressed through the links until reaching what we know as a Top Link Fireman post at Old Oak Common by 1890. In between times he would undoubtedly have fired on the Broad Gauge. At Old Oak we know he worked to Plymouth, lodging there overnight before returning to Paddington the next day. It was at his Plymouth lodgings in 1900, that he met, courted and later married Florence Pengelly, his lodging landlady's daughter, whereupon he brought his new bride back to reside at Hammersmith near to his home depot. Promotion to driver followed and to the comparative backwater of Bridgewater in 1910. It was at Hammersmith in 1901 that my father Owen Hatherell was born, one of three children. Sadly, following a short illness, Grandmother Florence died in 1910, leaving father the care of three young children.

Help came from family and friends, father meanwhile having been brought up surrounded by railway talk it not surprising to find that he too followed into a railway career. This was not however on the GWR, but instead with the Somerset & Dorset, which he joined around 1914/15 as a junior clerk in the Goods Office at Bridgwater. At that time his pay was 5/- per week. In 1916 father was transferred to the station at Blandford, dealing mainly with parcels of civilian clothing from new army recruits posted to the nearby camp and which were being sent back to their homes. Later, with the war almost over, he returned to his former clerk's role at Bridgwater although again shortly afterwards there was personal tragedy when grandfather and what

would have been my aunt, grandfather's daughter, were struck down with influenza. Both died within a few days of each other, my grandfather on the actual Armistice Day.

Meanwhile father's experience of the S & D was widening with a short period at Edington Junction and then by taking charge of clerical work at Ashcott and Shapwick. This was followed by a move to Glastonbury where my father Owen was married in 1926. I arrived in the world, named John Watts Hatherell, on 5th June 1929.

Father remained at Glastonbury until 1939, at which time he was offered the role of Relief Station Master and with it a return to Blandford. Promotion to a higher grade relief role, this time back at Glastonbury, came around 1943 and which meant covering the whole of the S & D plus certain LMS lines, Bath to Bristol, Bristol to Avonmouth and Mangotsfield to Gloucester. He even had a few days at Selly Oak!

With the formation of British Railways in 1948, opportunities to transfer were far greater than before and by 1953 father was looking towards a more settled life. Consequently he heard of, applied for and was successful at interview at Exeter for the vacant Station Master post at Bideford, which he took in early 1953. Father remained here until retiring after 49 years railway service, just before the Torrington line was closed in October 1965. He died, aged 80, in February 1981.

We are, though, jumping ahead somewhat, as I so well recall playing around the S & D railway as a boy. We would watch the trains at Midford, at times also assisting the signalman there in working the telegraph instruments and retrieving the all-important single line tablet, which an enthusiastic fireman of a down train had thrown on to the catcher but missed, instead falling down the side of the nearby

The genus for this article came from Richard Simmons - see Part 1 of ' Life at Southampton TSO', in Issue 6.

Richard suggested John Hatherell was a man well worth speaking to and it was he who then created the introduction.

John was most welcoming, a delight to speak to and most keen on seeing his recollections in print.

Sadly within a few days of that first interview, I received the news John had passed away.

There I assumed matters would end. That is until a telephone call from his wife June, that she would like to see the piece completed.

It is with grateful thanks to June Hatherell that we include this section, in memory of a enthusiastic and professional railwayman.

Father, Owen Hatherell's 'in post' at Bideford and his retirement letter from the same station in 1964.

embankment. On a number of occasions I have scrambled down the bank to retrieve that all-important piece of railwayana. So much we also took for granted, the through trains from the north to the south coast on summer Saturdays, the local passengers using the stations and of course the various types of different goods traffic; also the chocolate bars available from the machine on Bridgwater Station where Uncle Bob Ryan was a clerk. We would see the blue S & D Scammel 3-wheel lorry and trailer collecting and delivering on a regular basis, once I recall, with a coffin tied on to the back of the trailer.

By Christmas 1945, father, Owen Hatherell, was relieving at his home station of Glastonbury, S & D. I was by now 16 and had ambitions of becoming an electrical engineer. But a visit by the Divisional Civil Engineer from Exeter Queen Street would change all that, as in December 1945 I was offered the job of a temporary tracer in the Civil Engineer's office at Exeter. I accepted, even though this meant lodging at Exeter during the week and returning home at weekends. I have to admit company loyalty was not as great as practicalities when it came to getting home, for on a Saturday lunchtime after a five and a half day week, I would use the Great Western route from Exeter St Davids as far as Taunton, getting a bus from there to Glastonbury; far quicker than going by SR east from Exeter and changing at Templecombe. That is except on one occasion, when on arriving at St Davids I thought the train I needed was about to depart and rushed down the steps to jump on, only to find out it was first stop Gloucester. I was a bit late getting back that day.

At the time I joined the Southern, one of my first

jobs was to look after the Hallade recorder. With the office rather remote from Waterloo and always independent under W H Shortt, we had our own machine and did all the recording on the Division, which stretched from Wilton to Plymouth, Padstow and Ilfracombe, plus all the associated branch lines and of course the S & D between Bath and Broadstone. I was told that prior to my time in the office, Mr Shortt had the back seat of his car removed and ran it around Exeter with the Hallade recorder in the vehicle to test the suspension.

Working with the recorder in my early days was a very good way of getting a thorough knowledge of the area we covered. We were very proud of the high standard of the main line from Salisbury to Exeter, the technical staff working closely with the P/Way Inspectors and length gangs to maintain this excellence. We just knew ours was better than the GWR.

We also had a close relationship with the operating departments, including the drivers. I normally told the driver when we had the Hallade recorder on his train, sometimes with mixed results. In one case on the Brighton to Plymouth service, which we joined at Salisbury, I spoke to the driver on the 'West Country' who was renowned for fast running and who promised to give me 'a good run'. This certainly proved to be the case, for we clocked 103 mph in the dip just before Templecombe. I saw him at Exeter and learned it was his last trip before retiring. We presented him with a copy of the record.

Whilst at Exeter, late on Friday 31st January 1946, the office received notice that the local ganger from Shepton Mallet had seen ballast disappearing down a hole in Bath Road viaduct. This seemed impossible, but even so I was detailed to take various pieces of kit home with me on the Saturday and then, after the weekend, attend the viaduct on Monday, with instruments to check the levels. It was certainly not considered an immediate problem and it could not be imagined that anything serious could occur.

What I found out over the weekend, was that at 10.55 pm on the Sunday the centre pier of the viaduct had collapsed, carrying with it the piers on either side. This was on the side of the widened, not the original viaduct. Fortunately nothing had been crossing the spans at the time. Following inspection, trains were running again over the original section by the afternoon of the following day. Within 10 days all the rubble and damaged track had been removed, the ballast on the remaining single line and where there was of course no parapet, being held in place by timber baulks. Even so without the visual reassurance of a parapet in place, it must have been a worrying sight. One Bath driver, Vic Hunt, was reported as refusing to work over the structure in this state. Repairs were completed and both lines were finally restored to use in mid-September of the same year.

National service interrupted matters in 1947, although unlike many other railwaymen when called up, I was selected for the Royal Engineers and after initial square-bashing and then six months sapper training at Malvern, found myself at Longmoor looking after surveying equipment. At this time, Longmoor was viewed almost as a worldwide training centre for railway surveyors, although the training itself was orientated more towards new railway construction rather than maintenance. My job was to clean and service the theodelites and other equipment, sometimes returned covered in local sand. I was also fortunate at Longmoor in that I was allocated my own private accommodation billet and store, albeit small and it was in here that I undertook the necessary cleaning work.

Returning to the railway in 1949 I found there was now a girl, June Hocking, in the tracer's office, just one amongst ten men. It was my privilege to get to know

Above - *John Hatherell with survey gear at Longmoor, outside his 'office' and survey store, 1948/49.*

Possibly the same bridge work as seen previously, although John's note on the reverse refers to the Chard branch and 1955. Quite exactly what the Road Traffic Act would have made of this move can only be guessed at.

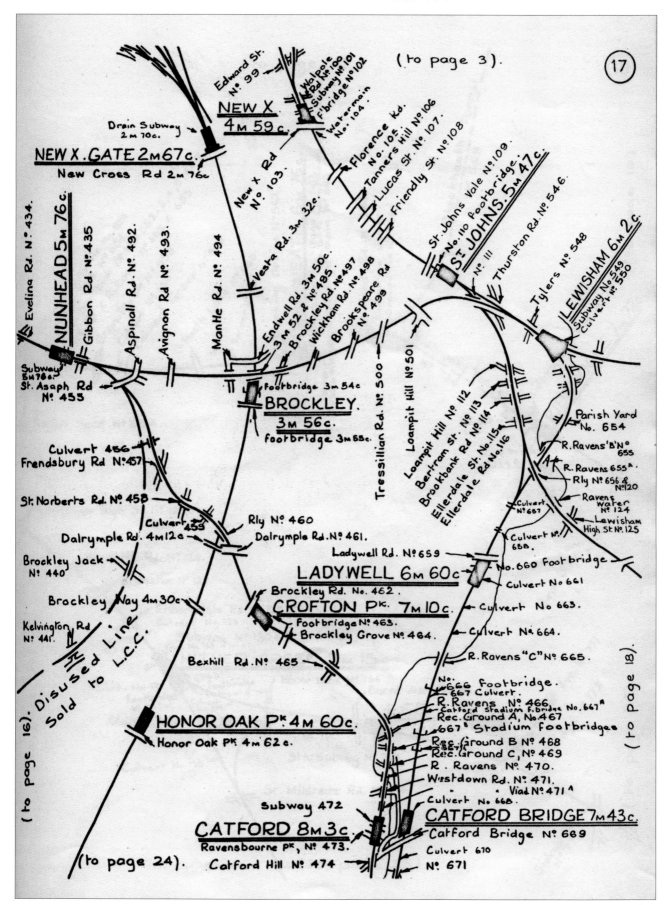

Left - *Part of the Bridge Map (Booklet) for London (Eastern) Division.*

Right - *Inside Stewarts Lane Bridge Shop in in 1964. The metalwork is a steel tunnel centre, designed by John whilst at Purley in 1962 and first used in Sevenoaks Tunnel.*

her and we were married in 1951. June was able to handle herself well in what was a primarily male environment, controlling the men when necessary as regards their otherwise sometimes colourful language.

In the early 1950s, changes to regional boundaries meant the Exeter office took over the former WR lines from Castle Cary southwards to Weymouth, as well as the route east from Dorchester to Hamworthy which included the Swanage branch. I recall it was at this time I first became involved in bridge work whereas before this I had been solely involved on the permanent way side of work.

The Exeter office closed in 1955, although before this I had applied for and been successful in gaining promotion, as I thought at the time, to Ipswich. Instead I was asked if I really wanted to leave the Southern and thus found myself on the staff of the Chief Civil Engineer's bridge design office at Deepdene. At the same time, June was offered promotion to Waterloo but in the event also ended up at Deepdene where she eventually became the head tracer.

My section boss at Deepdene, names had perhaps better not be mentioned, was a brilliant if eccentric character, renowned for resting at lunchtimes by lying flat-

out on his desk fast asleep. Whilst expert at all aspects of bridge theory, he was perhaps not the best practical man and consequently when discussing practical issues, I found it helpful to sometimes take in my Meccano to try out new ideas.

It was during my time at Deepdene that the Lewisham disaster of 4th December 1957 occurred which brought about the collapse of the adjacent flyover. We had the design for a temporary replacement structure worked out within two days, drawn by me and traced by June, indeed it was this that was subsequently built. This temporary replacement is still there more than half a century later.

Promotion came in 1959, to Bridge Assistant, at the District Engineer's Office, Purley. This office had responsibility for some 3,000 bridges in an area ranging from Redhill northwards-ish to Sevenoaks, east to Strood, the South London lines, as well the Brighton lines through Clapham and thence on to Victoria. In additional to bridges, we also had responsibility for metal station roofs. All this structural work covered inspection, maintenance and renewal. Rail bridges over the Thames were also included: they were scheduled for a thorough inspection at least once every five years.

Although the Southern maintained its own small bridge shop at Stewarts Lane, for major engineering work we would engage outside contractors. In charge of our office was Frank Prior, the type of leader who would not interfere. Instead he would leave his various sections to act appropriately, but trusted them to advise him should a problem develop.

I was by now also on call should an incident occur out of hours and I remember one particular occasion when an abnormal load being moved by road and despite having a Police escort, struck and fractured the supporting girder of an overbridge carrying the main line near Sevenoaks. Fortunately the GPO, as it was then called, were working nearby and had left a supply of new telegraph poles in connection with their work. We simply 'borrowed' one, which was then used to support the

Above - *Temporary trestling at St Johns, designed by John whilst he was based at Deepdene. John prepared the first pencil drawings over a weekend, working unpaid at home. These were then traced in ink onto linen by June on the kitchen table. The design was intended to last just 18 months with a permanent replacement provided in 1959. The decision to go ahead with a replacement was deferred, first in 1960, again 1968 and finally in 1972, when it was agreed the 'temporary bridge' should become 'permanent'. Even so, understandable maintenance and replacement of certain parts has been necessary.*

Left - *The key to the trestle drawings prepared by John and June. Both their initials appear shown.*

In later years, John assisted both the Isle of Wight Steam Railway and East Somerset lines when it came to forming connections with the BR network.

broken sections so allowing trains to resume, although at reduced speed.

Speaking of borrowed items, the various arches underneath places such as Waterloo, Cannon Street, South Bermondsey etc had long been used by both the railway and various businesses to store goods, including one at London Bridge, but I will not divulge exactly where, in which proof liquor was stored. We had occasion to enter some of these arches once, finding stored inside numerous items of stolen civil engineering equipment taken from work sites on the railway. Needless to say we borrowed all of our things back again. It just seemed a bit of a cheek to steal railway equipment and then store it in a railway arch.

Further promotion, in 1965, took me to the post of Assistant to the District Engineer (Planning and Work Study) at Eastleigh, at which point I was also assisting with the Bournemouth electrification. This included the conversion of the area around Bournemouth West to a maintenance depot for the new electric stock. Later a post was advertised for Area Civil Engineer Bournemouth with another similar vacancy on the South Eastern lines. As was the usual practice, I applied for both and was subsequently advised I had been successful in the Kent vacancy. A colleague, living in Kent, was advised he had been successful for Bournemouth. Fortunately common sense prevailed and I moved to the Bournemouth role, now covering an area from Weymouth to Southampton, east to Fareham, Romsey and the line north of Weymouth to just the other side of Dorchester West. This included all associated branch lines.

It was whilst in this role that I instigated various works including the design for the rebuilding of Redbridge viaduct, simplifying the layouts at Lymington Junction and Brockenhurst, as well as the major realignment of trackwork at Southampton Central in association with the resignalling there. At nearby Northam we encountered particular problems, for by realigning the curve to increase the speed limit slightly, we had to be careful we did not go beyond what it referred to as 'the optimum speed', meaning the speed at which the number of faster trains travelling quicker over a section of line starts to outstrip available line capacity, in this case at nearby Southampton Central, even if the latter location had by now been resignalled for bi-directional running. During the excavations for the new alignment at Northam, we also disturbed traces of settlements from earlier times including a number of rubbish pits. Even though we called in local experts, nothing of any major archaeological significance was found. Northam curve also saw an unusual incident in that consequently to the provision of a check rail due to the sharpness of the curve, the electrical return had twice the area of rail to travel through. This in turn was causing problems with the track-circuit impedance bonds at either end of the curve. One solution would have been to provide rail joints at more frequent intervals, but this would have upset the actual curvature, making it more like a series of straight lines. The solution found, was to fix a fourth rail

The original Redbridge Viaduct near Southampton prior to reconstruction. The replacement was another design by John produced whilst at Deepdene in 1958. The replacement still stands today. Ironically, some years later, when in post as Area Civil Engineer, Bournemouth, this same replacement would come under John's area of responsibility. Not mentioned in the text but included in some notes John had left for us, was the occasion when he was called out due to snow blocking Bincombe Tunnel near Weymouth. We may well assume this was the severe winter of 1963.

on the high side, so balancing the return current route. An added bonus was that as it was fixed to the sleepers, this extra rail also helped in keeping the curve in good alignment. I had first noticed this arrangement in use at Lewisham when involved with the 1957 disaster there.

Whilst based at Bournemouth I had use of a railway van for necessary call-outs. On one occasion (the circumstances for which are now long forgotten), I was driving the van along a country lane when a horse or pony appeared from the edge of the road ending up sitting on the bonnet of the van. There was no damage to the horse or me, I am glad to say, the former simply got up and wandered off, but not so the railway van, which displayed some evidence of the occurrence. I well recall when completing the accident report, there was a space for 'Horse Power of other vehicle involved'. Being based at Bournemouth, I was also accused at times of having a second part-time job, 'putting out deck-chairs'. This came about as I would tan easily, so giving the impression I spent all my days sunning myself rather than working. Such opportunities would not come for a while, although there was more time available for hobbies and interests after accepting early retirement in September 1984.

Mechanised Ballast Cleaning at Petts Wood

Introduction

The permanent way of any railway is dependent on a self-draining ballast layer and a good supporting formation.

The ballast allows water to get away from the track and provides a good medium to use to pack the track to the required vertical profile and hold it to the correct horizontal alignment. In the south of England ballast was often granite, although limestone, shingle and ash were also used. Even chalk was briefly tried, although this proved very unsuccessful, tending to coalesce around the sleepers, preventing free drainage and providing little support to the permanent way. Latterly, a single size of granite was usually used, as it was found to be robust and its angular nature locks together well to support the track. Using a single size of stone also ensures that there are gaps between individual stones for water to freely drain away from the track.

Below the layer of ballast lies the formation – the embankments and cuttings which level out the landscape for a railway line. Embankments were generally made out of whatever came out of the nearest cutting. Clay embankments are probably most common, although sometimes chalk or other broken rock or sand was used. Cuttings would simply be dug through whatever the local geology offered.

Over time, the formation tended to migrate into the ballast and contaminate it. If the formation was a sandy material, this could get worked into the ballast by the movement created by passing trains, where it would then block the gaps between individual pieces of ballast and prevent free draining of the track. Where poor formation exists today, it is usual to lay track on a geotextile membrane (which is rather like a thick blanket) to provide a physical barrier between the formation and the ballast and so reduce the degree of migration of material from the formation into the ballast.

To clean ballast which has become contaminated by the formation, without having to temporarily remove track which does not need renewal, a machine capable of cleaning the ballast beneath railway track was developed. This article examines one of the early ballast-cleaners, developed by the Matisa Company in the early 1950s for this purpose and the process it used.

The modern railways make extensive use of ballast-cleaning machines which essentially operate in a similar fashion to the machine described here, although the new High Output Ballast Cleaning Train operated by Network Rail is substantially larger than the Matisa machine!

The Ballast Cleaning Process

The ballast cleaner consists of a continuous chain of links shaped rather like hands, each with a number of protruding teeth which wrap underneath the track and dig the old dirty ballast to one side of the permanent way. This is then lifted up a chute by the same protruding teeth and is fed onto a series of large sieves or screens. These vibrate to sieve the ballast and remove any foreign matter, which is either deposited in a spoil train or left at the side of the track in the cess.

A cutter bar passes underneath the track to support the chain, keeping it in line. The chain is driven round at a steady rate, which is set to deliver the right volume of ballast to the screens and prevent overloading of the sieving mechanism. The track effectively hangs over the cutter bar and chain and in the early years of ballast cleaning the track was supported on wooden blocks once the cutter bar and chain had passed to allow clean ballast to flow back easily under the sleepers. Once the ballast cleaning machine had passed and the sorted clean ballast had been placed back around the sleepers, the track was 'rough packed' by hand to allow safe passage of a ballast train to top up the ballast with fresh clean stone.

Ballast which has become heavily contaminated with clay (often found in cuttings with poor drainage) is not suitable for cleaning by this process as it either sticks together when dry in a solid mass, or becomes very sticky when wet. In either case, the screens find it extremely difficult to sort good ballast from small lumps of clay and the return ballast to the track can be of very poor quality. Sometimes the local gang would dig trial holes in advance of the work between the sleepers and about a foot below the bottom of the sleeper. This was to investigate the condition of the ballast and formation so the suitability for ballast-cleaning or digging could be assessed.

Excavation of the entire ballast beneath a stretch of track could be achieved with these machines if track lowering was required. This process tended to produce large volumes of spoil as the screens are not used to separate reusable stone from waste. Instead, all the ballast dug out by the chain is deposited adjacent to the track or in the wagons of a spoil train and thence taken off site. If this process is employed, the track is usually allowed to drop on to the formation level of the track at the bottom of the cut once the ballast-cleaner has passed. Lowering and excavation is a very slow process, so lengths tackled would be smaller.

The ballast-cleaning process was very slow when using these machines and remained so until the advent of modern hydraulically-controlled high-output machines. These now incorporate lift trolleys or hydraulic rollers to hold the track above the formation once the ballast has been removed. However, these had yet to be developed when these photographs were taken and the photographs show the track being supported on jacks to prevent the cutter bar being crushed by the weight of the machine and the track. The use of blocks and hand packing as soon as possible behind the cutter bar can also be seen, again to provide as much support as possible to the track.

The first stage in cleaning the ballast of a particular section of track was to dig a trench across the track for the chain and cutter bar to be set up in. This was often dug during the week before a weekend possession and it was common to dig a trench under a sleeper (as the chain had to start below sleeper level) and then block the

sleeper up, to allow traffic to continue to run until the weekend. The chain was made so it could easily be dismantled or assembled by inserting or removing the pins that held it all together.

In later years a cut depth of approximately 9 inches was generally used beneath the bottom of the sleeper as this was the size of the teeth of the cutter chain on the machines and it would be angled for drainage to the cess. Earlier chains were slightly smaller. This depth gave a chain which was sufficiently strong for the task and created a good depth of new ballast, but did not require excessive energy to drive the chain through the dirty ballast. If you were prepared to make a few passes with the machine, almost any depth could be cut, but deeper

Matisa Ballast Cleaner No 2028 in operation on bullhead track fitted with a conductor rail. It is obviously of great interest to the senior management present! The cutter bar can be seen appearing below the sleeper and the cutter chain can be seen rising up out of the ballast, having crossed under the track. Dirty ballast is being pulled up the chute in the foreground. The man nearest the management is pushing the ballast forming the shoulder down either side of the track into the path of the chain, and others can be seen 'turning in' spilt ballast and preparing to put in wooden blocks to hold the track up once the ballast-cleaner has passed. These, together with a bit of packed loose stone, would hold the track up above the formation and allow the returned clean ballast to flow under and around the sleepers, with a bit of persuasion from a shovel. The front portion of the machine to the right of the group of gentlemen appears to be a separate piece of lifting equipment, with a powered jacking arrangement. A number of spare blocks can be seen stacked on the front of the machine, ready to be pushed in under the sleepers once the cutter bar and chain have passed.

cuts would produce significantly more spoil and an already slow process became very slow indeed!

Sometimes it would be necessary to 'spring' the track up in front of the machine to lift it slightly out of the ballast if the going was tough, or if there were under track obstructions such as cable routes or buried structures. Depth control was rudimentary on these early machines and the profile of the bottom of the cut generally followed the profile of the track. Platform walls, underbridges, level crossings, pointwork and so forth tended to prevent cleaning, although the track was sometimes slewed sideways where possible to get it away from bridge abutments and allow free passage of the ballast-cleaning machine.

The work was very dirty, noisy and dangerous; particularly as the power and hence speed of these machines evolved and increased. These photographs are interesting as they show an almost total disregard for the safety of the machine operators around a machine which had, even at this time, enough power to scoop solid ballast from under the track using cutting teeth which were designed to draw in ballast to the cleaner shoots, and would easily draw in a man's trouser leg if caught by mistake. Written instructions were issued setting out safe

Viewed from the other direction, the chain can now be clearly seen conveying the dirty ballast up the chute to the top of the machine ready to pass through the screens contained within it. As explained above, these would sieve the dirty ballast to separate stone of an acceptable size from the dirty ballast for return to the track. The name of the machine is really slightly misleading – it doesn't actually clean the individual pieces of ballast, but sieves them to remove fine material to improve the drainage of the track. It becomes much more difficult to get a ballast cleaner to work effectively when the ballast is wet as the fine material tends to stick to the ballast or clump together into lumps, which the sieves then treat as normal stone and return to the track. Clay areas are best avoided with a ballast cleaner as the machine cannot really distinguish between actual stone ballast and lumps of clay of a similar size that have stuck themselves together, and tends to return both to the track. The machine shown here seems so basic compared to the modern large high-output machines, but the basic process remains very similar. On this early machine the machine operator is on top of the machine which would make viewing the actual cut more difficult. The hoist mechanism in the middle of the machine would be used to lift the relatively heavy chain and cutter bar components into place. Lighting is primitive, but at least some was provided!

Viewed from above the machine, the screens and conveyor belts can be seen more clearly. The chute for the dirty ballast can clearly be seen rising from the right of the picture to the top of the machine. It then discharges dirty ballast on to the vibrating screens near the man on top. The screens are driven by the belt system visible above the oil drum. Modern machines incorporate further conveyors which process the ballast through extra inclined and vibrating screens. Clean ballast is dropped back on to the conveyor at the bottom left of the machine which returns it to the track. The foreign matter which has been screened out of the dirty ballast is moved along the conveyor seen rising on the left hand side of the photograph and was often spread along the bank, as is being done here. Piling dirty ballast on the bank often actually caused more problems than the ballast-cleaning solved by interfering with the drainage or inducing bank slips. The practice of spreading spoil from ballast-cleaning beside the line – although used for many years – has been generally discontinued now and the dirty spoil is usually removed from site by wagon. Note how the track is raised behind the machine. This was initially done on wooden blocks put in under the track using jacks. These remained in place until the cleaned ballast was spread back on the track behind the machine, when the blocks would be removed. At this point the local P/Way gang would take over the job of returning the track to its proper alignment and pack the track up on small pyramids of ballast. This would allow a train of hoppers to be slowly and carefully reversed over the site and flood it with ballast. Once this had been done the serious hand-packing started, or if you were lucky a tamping machine would pack the ballast in under the sleepers.

methods of operation of these machines, but sadly serious accidents plagued ballast-cleaners throughout their years of use. Gradually the machines became surrounded in cut-out mechanisms, safety pull-to-stop cords and so forth to offer some hope of protection to staff who got too near the cutting chain. Today it is almost impossible to access the cutting bar or chain while a ballast-cleaner is in action.

These photographs were taken during the very early development of ballast-cleaners, and at this stage the concept was clearly new and all were interested in the new equipment. The 'Top Brass' are present to closely observe, comment and suggest adjustments while avoiding getting their feet and clothes dirty!

This sequence of photographs was taken at Petts Wood in South London in November 1953. Interestingly, it appears that the formation in this area is poor, as the base of the shallow cutting is shored up with old rail and sleepers. It is likely that this soft ground has migrated into the ballast, hence ballast-cleaning is being carried out in this area.

The track here is seen after the ballast train has reversed over it and dropped ballast in the fourfoot between the rails and on the ends of the sleepers. To some extent the new ballast will have flowed under the sleepers which were packed up ready for it in the previous photograph. Only a couple of hoppers at the rear of the train had been unloaded by the time this photograph was taken and the gang has started pushing the clean ballast around from the mounds already unloaded prior to the next run with the hoppers. Occasionally a ballast-ploughing van was used on the conductor rail areas of the Southern Railway and a plough van appears to bring up the rear of this hopper train. However, ballast-ploughing was less accepted on the Southern as a method of moving ballast around than it was on other areas and often Supervisors preferred to get the men to move ballast around by hand. A neater job can be achieved by hand with less ballast left around the chairs and rails which a ballast-plough could not achieve. Ballast-ploughs were also found to sometimes push the conductor rail around, even though the actual plough was cut to clear this. The height of the plough was adjusted by the large capstan wheels in the van. Generally a plough height of approximately 3 inches above the rail was used, usually set by placing a wooden key on the rail head and lowering the plough onto this. Lowering the plough below this height could cause it to dig into the ballast and get caught in the dips and hollows of poor track and dipped joints. Small quantities of ballast that got under the wheels of the plough van were usually crushed under the running wheels, but it was not unusual for the plough and hoppers to ride over small piles of stone in the hope that they would drop back onto the rails again! Stories of how high a wheel lifted were a bit like the size of fish caught by fishermen and derailments of hoppers were certainly not uncommon when less experienced staff got it wrong. The men are easily identified here. The P/Way Supervisor stands to the right and he supervised, rarely actually getting involved. The ganger can be seen crossing the track with the cross level gauge and the rest did as they were told... most knew what would happen next and just quietly got on with it. The track gauge was a badge of office and only the ganger and Supervisor used it. By the time the track was shovel packed, checked for level (often by getting down and looking along the rail), and any dipped joints or track twists packed out of existence, the track could be reopened with a temporary speed restriction. The loaded ballast train would have helped to roll the new track into place by slowly passing back and forth in the process of the work.

COLOUR INTERLUDE

For our Colour Interlude in this issue, we are privileged to introduce some of Paul Cooper's images of the 1960s at Farnborough. Paul's black and white work, both SR and elsewhere, has been seen previously in 'Steam Railway' and 'Steam World', including wonderfully evocative images of Bulleid's at speed in the very last days of steam working.

Here though a gentler approach and part preparations for electrification at Farnborough Main, 6th October 1965. On page XX, ex 'River' class tank No 31803 is seen shunting in the remains of the goods yard just weeks away from withdrawal. The duty was the local daily down goods, which usually involved shunting at most stations to Basingstoke. Farnborough was probably busier than most yards because of the regular supplies of coal in mineral wagons for the Royal Aircraft Establishment. These were in turn picked up by the RAE's 0-4-0 Bagnall tank 'Invincible' (or was it a Hunslet?) that trundled the wagons through the streets of Farnborough to the airfield until April 1968. There's an extensive coal pile in the yard as there was a Corrall's or Charrington's general coal distribution depot there.

Shortly afterwards the peace is broken as 34023 'Blackmore Vale' crosses from the Up main to Up slow on the approach to the station with a Bournemouth line service - notice the green 'GUV' as the first vehicle behind the tender. It was a comparatively rare event to do this at Farnborough as the train was certainly not stopping. Note that by now No 31803 had worked her way into the headshunt here.

Diesel photo – this is 'Crompton' D6548 and 'Hymek' D7021 portraying the differing styles of motive power and of course transmission type, favoured by the Southern and Western regions respectively. The former on a down freight, the latter on ballast empties in the goods bay platform. Note the stack of insulators for the electrification. You can see in the background the Cupola Dome of St Michaels Abbey, the home of the exiled Louis Napoleon and his wife the Empress Eugenie from the 1870s.

Finally above, 34066 'Spitfire' on a through load of empty ballast empties occupying the down slow line – note the Hymek is not on the empties in the bay at this stage. That was to happen later when I think she worked in light engine to pick these up. Not that common an occurrence actually, as most workings were Cromptons or Warships (these on Exeter passenger workings of course). In the background, the lower quadrant arms are almost in their last days, they like almost everything else in the illustrations, would soon be consigned to history.

'Hymek' in the bay with the driver cleaning the windscreen and on the up side D3044 is shunting more ballast wagons (- do we really care if it was an '08' or '09'?). As this was mid-electrification / track relaying, I suspect the forthcoming weekend was going to be one where the line was fully or partially closed for extensive work – those Sundays when steam services were diverted over 'The Alps'. Note the covered overbridge between the up and down sides, the cover was removed in the 70's. And, of course, not an orange vest in sight.

(Part of Paul Cooper's historic archive, 'Romsey LSWR, Industry, Enterprise and Family History', appeared in 'Southern Way No 5'.)

Issue No 8 of THE SOUTHERN WAY (ISBN 978 1 906419 18 9) will be available on 1st October 2009

To receive your copy the moment it is released, order in advance from your usual supplier, or direct from the publisher:

Kevin Robertson (Noodle Books) PO Box 279, Corhampton, SOUTHAMPTON, SO32 3ZX

Tel / Fax 01489 877880

www.noodlebooks.co.uk
www.kevinrobertsonbooks.co.uk

Please note due to circumstances outside our control, the cover price for single issues of
THE SOUTHERN WAY has had to rise to £12.95 with effect from this issue.